W9-BOF-651

MORE
CHAMPIONSHIP TEAMS
OF THE NFL

Exciting accounts of five outstanding football teams
and their championship seasons:
the 1967 Green Bay Packers, the 1968 New York Jets,
the 1970 Baltimore Colts, the 1971 Dallas Cowboys
and the 1972 Miami Dolphins.

MORE
CHAMPIONSHIP TEAMS
OF THE NFL

BY PHIL BERGER

illustrated with photographs

RANDOM HOUSE · NEW YORK

PHOTOGRAPH CREDITS: John E. Biever: 95; Vernon J. Biever: 21; Malcolm Emmons: 25, 31, 37, 74, 79, 82, 124, 146; Emmons & Brockway: 28–29; Ken Regan (Camera 5): endpapers, 2, 7, 8, 52, 64, 67, 69, 111; Al Satterwhite (Camera 5): 132; United Press International: 16, 34, 41, 61, 87, 99, 104, 118, 120, 129, 137, 142; Wide World Photos: 11, 44–45, 48, 92, 112, 115.
Cover: photo by Vernon J. Biever.

Copyright © 1974 by Random House, Inc. All rights reserved under International and Pan-American Copyright Conventions. Published in the United States by Random House, Inc., New York, and simultaneously in Canada by Random House of Canada Limited, Toronto. Manufactured in the United States of America.

Library of Congress Cataloging in Publication Data
Berger, Phil. More championship teams of the NFL. (Punt, pass, and kick library)
SUMMARY: Describes the championship seasons of the Green Bay Packers, New York Jets, Dallas Cowboys, Baltimore Colts, and Miami Dolphins.
1. National Football League—Juvenile literature. [1. National Football League. 2. Football] I. Title.
GV955.5.N35B42   1974   796.33'264'0973   74-4199
ISBN 0-394-82767-8   ISBN 0-394-92767-2 (lib. bdg.)

To my nephew
Danny Milkman

Contents

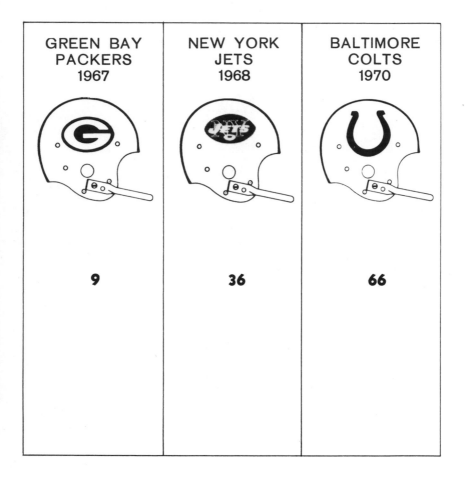

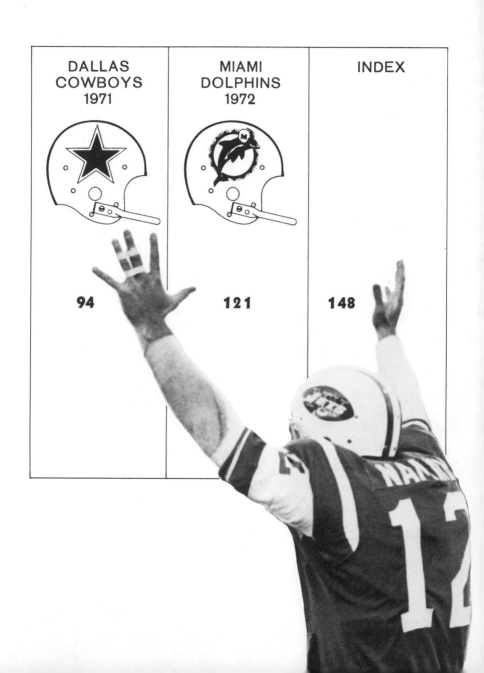

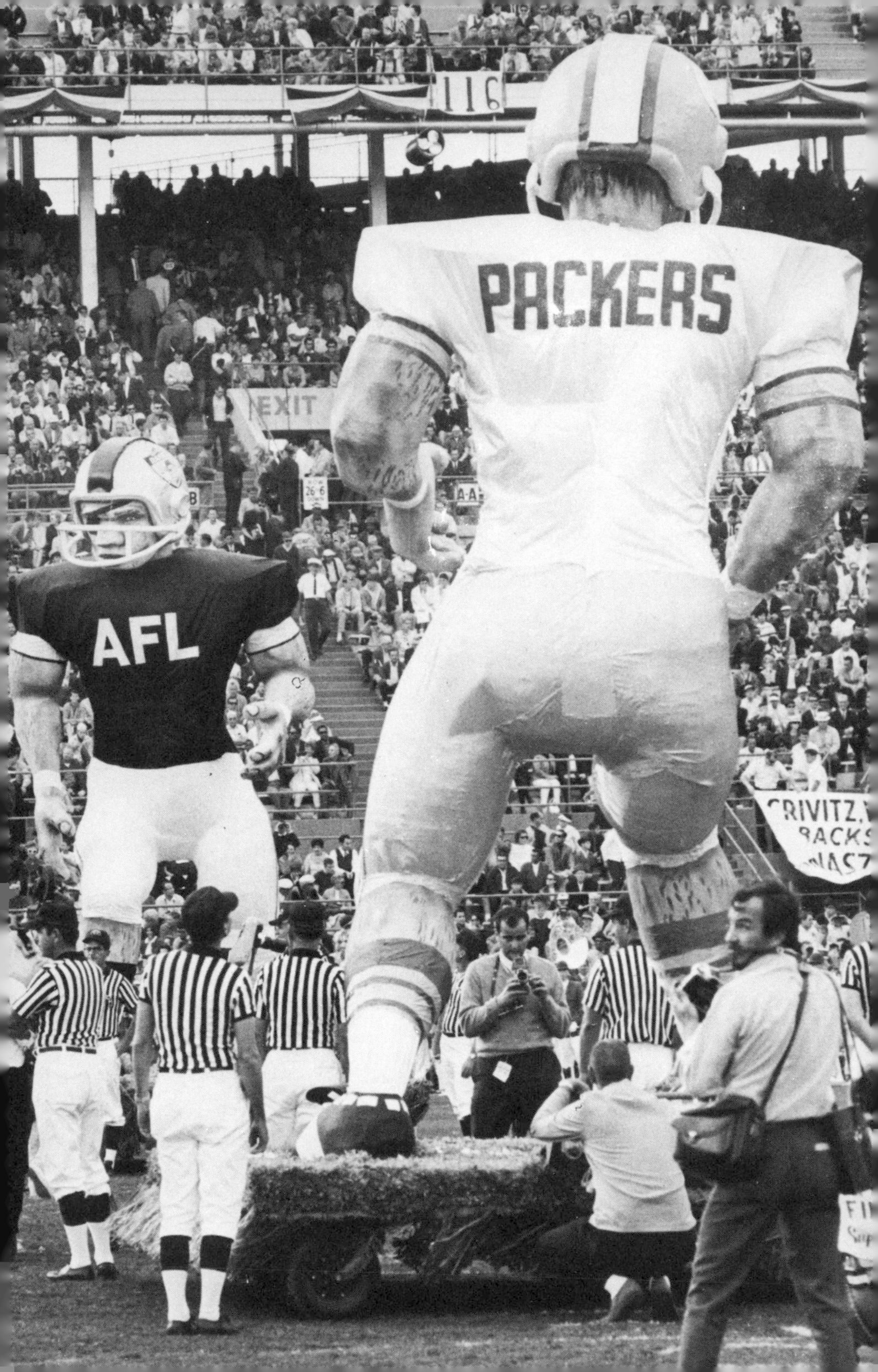
116
PACKERS
AFL
EXIT

Green Bay
Packers
1967

It was not the kind of start their fans expected. But Detroit 17, Green Bay 17 was all the Packers could manage in the opening game of the 1967 season.

For many it seemed a sign of the times. In the last eight years the Packers had dominated pro football, capturing five Western Conference titles, four NFL championships and one Super Bowl crown. But all that was history. In 1967 the word on Green Bay was that an era was at an end. The Pack, it was said, was no longer a major football power.

In many ways, the 1967 Packers did not look like the Green Bay teams of the past. Gone was the dynamic running duo of Paul Hornung and Jim Taylor, and with them had gone some of the sock in the Packer attack.

Other players who had sparked the great Green Bay dynasty were still there, but they were aging. Stars like Willie Davis, Forrest Gregg, Bob Jeter, Henry Jordan, Jerry Kramer, Max McGee, Ray Nitschke, Bob Skoronski, Bart Starr, and Willie Wood were all at least 30 years old. Even their fans wondered how long they would keep going.

Fortunately, one thing remained the same in Green Bay. The man running the Packers was still Vince Lombardi, and that made up for a lot in the world of pro football. In his long and noisy reign at Green Bay, Lombardi had changed the Packers from the league patsies they had been in 1958 to perennial contenders. But Green Bay's glory was slated to end with the '67 season, when Lombardi would retire from coaching after the final game. Lombardi, to be sure, wanted that game to be in Miami—the site of the Super Bowl.

So the season had the added importance of being Lombardi's last stand. And for the veterans it was the final triumph to be had under the coach. To win the Super Bowl one last time would be the only fitting climax to the Lombardi era.

Lombardi's winning philosophy was quite simple. "Knock people down," he told the Packers. "That's what the game is about." Lombardi stressed the principles of quick-hit football—blocking and tackling. There was nothing fancy about the way Packer teams played the game—nothing fancy but their winning records.

Coach Vince frets as the Pack fights it out on the field.

It took great persuasion to make a team perform the way Green Bay did. Lombardi, a feared but admired taskmaster, pushed his players to their limit. "I am restless, worrisome, demanding, sometimes impatient and hot-tempered," Lombardi once said, and while those traits hardly qualified him for the priesthood he sought as a boy, they served him well in the NFL.

As one of the Packers explained, "You never hear us call him Vince. It's always Coach Lombardi or Mr. Lombardi."

Lombardi was almost a god-like figure to Green Bay players and fans. But although he encouraged that kind of awe and respect, he never lost his sense of perspective—or his sense of humor. Once, at a practice session, he swatted a bee that was buzzing about him. The bee, quite naturally, returned. Afterward, Lombardi told reporters with just a trace of a smile, "I got stung on the back of the neck during practice today. The bee died."

On the field, however, Lombardi was all business. "He chews you out and you don't like it," said tackle Jordan. "But he gets the message across. He runs a tight ship on and off the field, and he's right."

Lombardi kept his distance from the Packers and never allowed sentiment to influence his judgment. When a player was no longer useful to the team, that man went. But as with all matters concerning Lombardi, it was never quite that simple. For instance, when Packer blocking guard Jerry Kramer reported to training camp one year after undergoing eight stomach operations, his football days seemed numbered. Lombardi, however, was so worried about Kramer's pension rights that he discussed the problem with pro football commissioner Pete Rozelle.

"He'll never be able to play," Lombardi told Rozelle, "but I want to keep his pension rights alive. How can I do it?"

"Let him come to training," Rozelle said. "Put him on the taxi squad or something. We'll work out some way to protect him."

But Jerry Kramer proved a man after Lombardi's own heart. He needed no special favors. He made the team on his own merits. And in 1967, Jerry Kramer symbolized the never-say-die spirit of Green Bay.

So despite their opening day disappointment, the Packers looked forward to their second game of the year. With guys like Kramer blocking, the Packers opened gaping holes against Chicago. Through those holes ran fullback Jim Grabowski for 111 yards in 32 carries. Place-kicker Don Chandler contributed a 48-yard field goal, and the Packers wound up with a 13–10 win. But even in victory all was not well with the Pack. For that afternoon Green Bay made the kind of mistakes that drove Lombardi wild—five interceptions thrown by quarterback Bart Starr and three fumbles by Grabowski.

Even though they had won the game, Lombardi had

nothing but harsh words for Green Bay's performance. His post-game outburst came as no surprise to the dejected Packers, who knew from past experience how their coach felt about sloppy play.

Rookie running back Travis Williams had recently learned—the hard way—how Lombardi dealt with mistakes. Williams, who could run the 100-yard dash in 9.3 seconds, had the kind of speed the Packers needed. But in training camp he had repeatedly fumbled the football, an evil that Lombardi would not tolerate. "Two different times he told me he didn't want to ever see me without a football in my hands, so I'd get better acquainted with it," Williams recalled. "He meant downtown, uptown, at practice, the drugstore while eating, and I don't know if that included bed, but I took one there just to be safe. Mr. Lombardi, he means what he says, you know."

Coach Vince made it gospel in Green Bay that mistakes cost. As teammate Henry Jordan told Williams, "Around here we don't think of this as football. It's a loaf of bread worth $30,000 a man. You don't drop that kind of bread, and you don't get fancy with it. Be fast, don't be fancy—and don't fumble!"

And that wasn't the end of it, either. Just to make sure that Williams got the point, reserve quarterback Zeke Bratkowski had outfitted a ball with handles shaped from tape and handed it to the rookie. Williams got the message. "I learned they don't want fumbling around Green Bay," he said.

Like Williams, the Packers all learned from their mistakes. And how they learned! After their mistake-filled game against Chicago, the Packers operated like a smooth-running machine when they faced Atlanta the next week.

The Packers did all that Lombardi required—and more. They blocked and tackled, and played with pride. Bart Starr was out of the game with an injury, but even that didn't stop Green Bay. Zeke Bratkowski, filling in at quarterback, was a star in his own right. In the first half he threw touchdown passes of 5 and 50 yards to Carroll Dale.

Then the defense—Lombardi's pride and joy—took over. First, defensive end Willie Davis smashed through the Falcon line to tackle Atlanta quarterback Randy Johnson for a safety. And then the whole Pack came on, with middle linebacker Ray Nitschke making his routinely bone-cracking tackles time after time. At 6-foot-3 and 240 pounds, the bald and bruising Green Bay veteran packed quite a wallop. And as the middle linebacker, Nitschke was always in the thick of battle.

On that afternoon he led the Packer defense in a thorough rout of Atlanta. By the end of the game the Falcons had gained a paltry 58 yards, as Green Bay ran away with a 23–0 victory. But Atlanta was just an expansion team in its second year of existence, and no real test for the Packers.

A club like the Detroit Lions was another thing altogether. It was the Lions that Green Bay faced the

Green Bay's big Jim Grabowski crashes through the fierce Lion line.

following week. Detroit had already held the Pack to a tie in the season's opener, and the Lions came out roaring the second time around. By the end of the first quarter Detroit had run up a 10–0 lead.

But Lombardi's team did not quit. And that afternoon was no exception. After a slow start Green Bay finally began to move. Jerry Kramer, still going strong after all the injuries he'd suffered, opened the holes for the ground game. After ten years in pro football his body was covered with so many scars and stitches that his teammates called him "Zipper."

With the running game established, Bratkowski took to the air. First he threw a 19-yard touchdown pass to Donny Anderson. Later on, he tossed a 13-yarder to Boyd Dowler for another TD. To top it all off, Nitschke intercepted a Lion pass and scrambled 19 yards for the score. By the end of the game Green Bay had racked up a 27–17 victory.

Bratkowski was doing an excellent job in Starr's absence. But the followup week he ran up against the fierce pass rush of the Minnesota Vikings. In the fourth quarter of that game, he threw two interceptions that resulted in one field goal and one touchdown for the Vikings—and a 10–7 loss for the Packers.

Back to the action came the recovered Starr—and none too soon. Although the Pack (3–1–1) was leading Chicago 2–3 in the battle for the Central Division crown, it was too early in the season to take anything for granted—particularly with a Green Bay team whose age might show late in the stretch.

Nevertheless, with Starr back again, the Packers couldn't help thinking of victory. For it was Bryan Bartlett Starr who had led the Packers to glory in past years. In the rough world of pro football Starr seemed gentler than most. Quiet and softspoken off the field, he was tough enough when it counted.

"There is a softness in him," said Jerry Kramer. "A sort of gentle manliness. But there is also an iron-hard spirit. When we were playing the Bears about five years ago, Bill George came through and hit Bart in the mouth. A real good shot. Blood all over. 'That'll take care of you, kid,' George said. You should have seen Bart. He snarled right back. Challenged him right there. That's one thing about this game. You have to be ready to fight, and Bart always is."

Starr brought that fight to Yankee Stadium against the New York Giants. For a while, though, it looked like a losing battle. By half time Green Bay trailed 14–10.

Then Starr began putting the attack together. Although Hornung and Taylor were gone, Starr still had Grabbo—big Jim Grabowski—to carry the football. And Grabowski ran as hard as a man could, busting through the holes opened by his blockers. And when Grabowski wasn't lugging the ball, Elijah Pitts was.

Pitts started a Packer rally in the third quarter with a

6-yard touchdown run. After that, Green Bay devastated New York. The Packers ran and passed with the kind of power encouraged by Lombardi. Nothing fancy. They just knocked the Giants silly. Green Bay scored 38 points in a wild second half for a catch-up 48–21 win.

It wasn't just the veterans that kept the Packer drive going, though. In the Pack's next game against St. Louis, a rookie led the way. It was Travis Williams, the speedster who'd had trouble holding onto the football earlier. With Herb Adderley nursing a sore shoulder, Lombardi put Williams in to return a kickoff against the Cardinals in the fourth quarter.

Green Bay was trailing 23–17 when Williams got his hands on the football. And this time he held on tight. Then he ran like blazes. No St. Louis player could touch him as he flew 93 yards for the touchdown, sparking a 31–23 comeback win. "Nice job," said Lombardi.

It was music to the rookie's ears. A few words from the coach sounded like a hallelujah chorus to Williams after all the time he had spent on the bench.

The Packers suffered a setback in their next outing, a 13–10 loss to Baltimore. But a week later Travis got the team back on the right track again. Against Cleveland he took Lou Groza's opening kickoff on Green Bay's 13 and streaked along the right sideline behind his blockers. Then he saw daylight, suddenly veered to the left slightly, and ran 87 yards for the touchdown.

That was just the beginning. Later in the first quarter,

Williams fielded a kick on his own 15 and once more raced toward his wedge. As he had done earlier, he again broke to his left. This time he had to slip by several tacklers before he could break into the clear. Only one Brown, Mike Howell, had a good tackling angle on Williams. But Travis managed to outrace him to the goal line for his second touchdown of the day, an 85-yard run. Ignited by Williams, Green Bay went on to hand the Browns the worst defeat in their history, 55–6.

Williams' great day against Cleveland made him an instant celebrity in Green Bay. Because of his speed, fans began calling Williams "The Roadrunner." A local automobile dealer, whose line included a car by that name, gave him a shiny new red one. Emblazoned on both sides in all colors of the rainbow were decals of that ridiculous bird.

But Williams got an even better gift from Vince Lombardi—a place on the Packers as the team's regular kick-returner. And then a strange thing began to happen. Kickoffs to Green Bay were squibbed far short of Williams. Opposing teams preferred to give Green Bay possession on its 35- or 40-yard line rather than risk having the Roadrunner—or Traveling Travis, as he was also known—sprint all the way for a touchdown.

That was okay with the Packers. For Green Bay was a team that made the best of its chances. Lombardi's clubs were relentless. When he first came to Green Bay in 1959 Lombardi had told them, "This is a game won

Speedy Travis Williams shows why he's called "The Roadrunner."

in here"—and he'd thumped his big fist against his heart.

Over the years Green Bay had had the heart. As a team, its men were known as "money players"—guys who played their best in clutch situations. And the Packers were always a team. Green Bay fortunes never rose and fell on one man. Lombardi had had great individuals—Hornung and Taylor were all-time NFL stars—but the Pack was first and foremost an outfit that pulled together.

It was truly a team effort that kept Green Bay going during the long '67 season. When the Packers lost running back Elijah Pitts to injuries, Donny Anderson came through as his replacement. So did Zeke Bratkowski, playing for the ailing Starr. Against the San Francisco 49ers, Anderson ran the ball for 89 yards—and Bratkowski ran the team! The second-string quarterback led the Pack to a 13–0 victory.

It was a tribute to Lombardi that the reserves had come through. Any man who played for the coach knew he had to be ready whenever he was needed. It didn't matter whether the player was an All-Pro like Nitschke or an NFL castoff like fullback Chuck Mercein.

Lombardi's Packers were like the New York Yankee baseball teams in their glory years, or the Boston Celtics under Red Auerbach. Those teams would pick up another team's discard and he would suddenly perform. Old Johnny Mize hit home runs for the Yankees long after the experts said he was all washed up. And Don Nelson had done little for the Los Angeles Lakers, but he was a shooting and rebounding whiz with the Celtics. Both of those teams had a winning tradition that seemed to bring out the very best in their players.

Green Bay had that same tradition. Paul Hornung had been ready to quit pro football before Lombardi came to Green Bay. But Hornung's career had peaked under the coach. Lombardi's magic had done that to others who had come to Green Bay too. Mercein, cut by two teams in one season (first New York and then Washington), was the latest of the NFL discards to end up in Green Bay, hoping the Packer magic would rub off on him.

The miracle had already happened to Travis Williams. The fumbling rookie had been transformed into a sure-handed kick-returner. In fact, it was the amazing Roadrunner who set up the go-ahead touchdown against the Chicago Bears in the Packers' next contest.

With the score tied 7–7 Williams took the ball and zigzagged through the Bear tacklers, sprinting 69 yards to the Chicago 25. Then Green Bay drove to the one-yard line, and Donny Anderson muscled the ball in from there. The Packers' 17–13 win over Chicago clinched first place in the West's Central Division for Green Bay.

Their place in the playoffs assured, the Packers slumped through the remaining regular-season games, losing two of their last three contests. In the season's finale Green Bay practically *gave* Pittsburgh its 24–17 victory by losing the ball three times on interceptions and six times on fumbles. Packer fans said it was only because the game meant nothing in the league standings. When it came time to play for the Western Conference championship, they vowed, the Pack would be back.

In past years the Packers had always been at their best in playoff games—but it would be harder in '67. To win the championship this time it would take three playoff victories—one more than needed in other years. That was because of the new breakdown of the Western Conference into two divisions. To earn the conference crown, Green Bay would first have to defeat the Los Angeles Rams—the Coastal Division leaders and the hottest team in all of pro football.

The Rams, led by quarterback Roman Gabriel, had won their last eight games of the season. Included among their victims was Green Bay, in the next-to-last game of the season. The Rams had won that one like the champions they were—with the big play. Late in the game LA's Tony Guillory had blocked Donny Anderson's punt. Then, with only 34 seconds left to play, Gabriel had thrown a touchdown pass to Bernie Casey to eke out the Rams' 27–24 victory.

The Rams would be trying for a repeat performance in the playoffs, but Green Bay was a team geared for the big ones. Before 49,861 fans at Milwaukee County

Against the Rams, Jerry Kramer (64) clears the way for Donny Anderson (44).

Stadium the Packers gave the LA upstarts a football lesson. And they did it in Lombardi's knock-em-sock-em way. In the lines, the starting place for Green Bay football, the edge clearly belonged to the Packers. The fierce execution that had always marked Green Bay line play under Lombardi was still there. No tired bones in "the pit," where the super-linemen dueled. Green Bay's lines—offense and defense—outplayed the Rams all afternoon.

When the Rams had the football, they couldn't move it—not with the incredible pressure put on by the Packer front four—Davis, Ron Kostelnik, Jordan, and Lionel Aldridge. The Green Bay defense kept barreling by the Ram blockers, bottling up the LA attack. Gabriel in particular had a bad time of it. All season he had made the plays to bail the Rams out, but now he seemed powerless. Green Bay's defenders never let up.

While Green Bay's defensive line kept up the pressure, Nitschke and the other linebackers sometimes stormed into the LA backfield on blitzes, hoping to get the quarterback. The Packers got Gabriel—and good. Five times that day they caught him with the football and unceremoniously dumped him to the turf. He never had a chance.

Meanwhile, Bart Starr, the Packers' gentleman-quarterback, was making a good case for the over-30 set. Working behind the powerful blocking of Jerry Kramer, Starr riddled the Ram defense. He completed 17 of 23 passes for 222 yards and a touchdown to Carroll Dale.

Starr had plenty of help from the Roadrunner, Travis Williams, who was having another of his dazzling games. In the regular-season game against the Rams, Travis had taken a kickoff four yards deep in the end zone and gone 104 yards for a touchdown, his fourth of the season on a kickoff return.

Now in the conference championship game he proved his performance was no fluke. The fleet-footed Williams, pressed into action as a starter, rushed for 88 yards and two touchdowns, one of them a brilliant 46-yard score. Travis had learned Lombardi's lessons— and more. After the game, a convincing 28–7 win for Green Bay, Packer fans hefted Williams to their shoulders and paraded him around the field in a gleeful demonstration. "It was like sitting up on a cloud and all the stars were shining," said Williams.

But the Packers weren't ready to celebrate yet. They still had to defeat Dallas for the league crown. The NFL championship game was played on December 31 at Lambeau Field in Green Bay. It promised to be the kind of brutal late-season contest that was standard in northern climates. The temperature at daybreak was 16 degrees below zero, and by game time it had "warmed up" to 13 below.

Both teams came well prepared. Green Bay pass-catcher Boyd Dowler packed a pair of little cotton gloves. Throughout the game, he'd slip them on during time-outs, and then stick them under his belt when play resumed. Other players braved the frigid day dressed in

Their freezing fans cheer the Pack on during the NFL championship game.

sweat shirts, thermal underwear, and woolen socks. It was an afternoon more suitable for arctic exploring than football.

But with so much at stake, the players had more on their minds than the weather. A win here meant a chance for the $15,000-a-player Super Bowl money. To the Packers it meant more than that—it also meant a chance to become the first team in NFL history to win three consecutive league championships. That would make Lombardi's Green Bay dynasty the greatest in pro football history. And, of course, whatever the outcome, it would be Lombardi's last year as coach—no small consideration for the Packers.

In the land of the Pack, sub-zero weather was not unusual, and Green Bay had a special subterranean electric heating system designed to keep the field in shape on the coldest of days. This time, however, it failed, and the ground froze up like an ice cube.

Before 50,861 shivering fans the Packers charged onto the field, determined to do Lombardi proud. Before the game started, Clint Murchison, the millionaire owner of the Dallas team had predicted, "It is too cold for the Green Bay passing game, and we will win with our running."

But 1967 had been a bad year for the "experts" and a fine year for Green Bay. Considered too old to keep up with the NFL young bloods, the Packers had already made it to the title game. Too cold to pass the ball? On Green Bay's first drive, Starr threw four completions in five passes, the last of them for 8 yards and a touchdown to Dowler.

Despite the icy cold the Packers had come out steaming. But Dallas did not buckle the way the Rams had. Even after Starr threw a second touchdown pass to Dowler, a 43-yarder, the Cowboys hung in. Their defense, especially Dallas' big front four (Jethro Pugh, George Andrie, Willie Townes, and Bob Lilly) began to come on. Even the Packers' great blockers couldn't keep them at bay.

In the second quarter the Cowboys got to Starr. Townes crashed into the Green Bay quarterback like a truck wiping out a roadblock. Down went Starr—and with him went the ball, bouncing away. Townes couldn't scoop it up, but Andrie was just behind him. The big Dallas defenseman grabbed the ball and ran in for the touchdown. A Dallas field goal chopped the Packer lead to 14–10 by half time. No question about it: The old men of Green Bay were in for a long, hard afternoon.

It was so cold on Lambeau Field that half-time entertainment had to be cancelled when the brass band instruments were made inoperative by the frosty weather.

Back on the field for the second half, the Dallas defense was making things hot for the Pack—especially

Bart Starr, Green Bay's veteran quarterback, calls the signals.

Bart Starr. Eight times that day the Green Bay quarterback got sacked by the Cowboy front four. The momentum had clearly switched to Dallas. As the scoreless third quarter ended, it seemed only a matter of time before the Cowboys would catch the Packers.

On the first play of the fourth quarter Dallas did just that. The Cowboys went ahead on a tricky Dallas play—a pitch-out to halfback Dan Reeves. As a college quarterback at South Carolina, Reeves had been an adept thrower. Now he lofted a perfect pass from midfield. Cowboy pass catcher Lance Rentzel caught it alone on the 20 and went in to score: Dallas 17, Green Bay 14.

Green Bay's dreams of glory were getting dimmer by the minute. The spark had gone out of the Pack. Cowboy defensive pressure remained fierce. In the last quarter the Packers could not seem to score. First Dallas forced the Packers to punt the ball. Then the Cowboys harassed Starr so much that Green Bay was forced to try a long-shot field goal from the 40. It missed.

With only 4:54 to play, the Packers gained possession for what might well be their last chance. "The ball was on the 32," recalled Jerry Kramer. "And I was thinking, 'Well, maybe this is the year we don't pull it off, that it will all end here.' But I know every guy made up his mind that we were going to go down swinging."

On the first play, Starr threw to Anderson for a six-yard gain. Then Chuck Mercein, in at fullback, made seven yards to give the Packers a first down on their own 45. Starr's next play was a pass—good to Dowler at the Dallas 42 for another first down.

The Packers were finally on the move. Or were they? For once again Townes roared into the backfield like a tank to wipe out Donny Anderson for a nine-yard loss. Still, the Packers didn't give up.

With the Cowboy defense back to protect against the long pass, Starr made use of the only alternative left him—the short-yardage pass. Twice he threw to Anderson—for twelve yards to the Dallas 39 and then, on third down, for nine more yards and a first down at the 30. The clock was down to just two minutes now.

Starr stayed with his secondary receivers on the pass. He hit Mercein for another 19 yards to the Dallas 11. Mercein, the same man who had been cut by New York and Washington, was about to become a Packer hero. He had been injured earlier in the game, but he played tough. Mercein showed just how tough he was on the next play.

From the 11 he bulled and twisted his aching bones to the Cowboy 3. Then Anderson drove to the one for the first down. But time was running out. Less than one minute—and one yard—stood between the Pack and victory. Anderson ran the ball into the thick of the Dallas line, but the Cowboy defense stood fast. No gain. The clock was still ticking; only half a minute remained.

Down to their knees went the Dallas front four again. Cowboy linebackers pounded them on their shoulder pads, urging them to hold the line. With time running out, Starr didn't linger over the signals. The ball was snapped right away. Again the lines crunched together, and again Anderson tried to move the football. This time he slipped, and before he could regain his footing, the Cowboys had swarmed all over him. Again, no gain.

The Packers called a time out. They still trailed 17–14, and now only 16 seconds remained. Green Bay had only two options: try a field goal to tie the game—or run a play from scrimmage to win or lose it.

Starr (15) scores the winning TD, and the Packers are NFL champs again.

Lombardi decided to bid for the victory, a decision quite in keeping with his hard-nosed football theories. With Coach Vince there was no wavering. The game was straight-ahead.

And straight-ahead went Starr under Lombardi's order. The call was for Starr to carry the football right through a designated hole that Jerry Kramer was to make. If Kramer got the job done, Starr would see daylight—and the Packers would have another NFL championship. But if he failed, Starr would go crashing into Jethro Pugh—and the Green Bay dynasty would come tumbling down.

But Kramer did what Green Bay players always did in the Lombardi years. He came through in the clutch. Ramming his shoulder into Pugh's bulk, he shoved the Dallas defender back and to the left. The hole was there, and Starr slid right through for the touchdown—and Green Bay's third straight NFL title.

Next stop: Super Bowl! The Packers went on to Miami to play against the AFL champions from Oakland, but the meeting was almost anticlimactic. Green Bay won it easily in a 33–14 rout.

For years afterward Packer fans proudly recalled the 1967 season and the glory that was Green Bay. And it was not of Super Sunday in Miami that they spoke, but of the one-yard line at frigid Lambeau Field, where Coach Vince made his real last stand. And what a beauty it was!

New York Jets 1968

When New York Jets owner Sonny Werblin signed a quarterback named Joe Namath back in 1965, he said, "I don't know how to define star quality, but this guy has it. When he comes into a game, people move to the edge of their seats."

No question about it. When Joe Willie Namath played, anything seemed possible. The flashy quarterback gave the American Football League and the Jets something they had not had before—the kind of excitement that packed ball parks.

The American Football League had come into existence in 1960. Although it was supposed to be a competitor for the established National Football League, in its early seasons the new league was certainly

inferior. Still, any league with a man who could throw a football the way Namath did couldn't be all bad.

In his first three seasons with the Jets, Namath threw 18, 19, and 26 touchdown passes. In 1967 alone, he completed 258 of 491 passes for an incredible league record of 4,007 yards.

Still, there were many people—especially NFL fans— who claimed not to understand what all the fuss was about. To them the Jets—even with Namath—were just another poor AFL team, hardly capable of beating the really good NFL clubs. In fact, Joe and the Jets weren't doing all that well in their own league. Their record was 5–8–1 in 1965, 6–6–2 in '66 and 8–5–1 in '67.

But the Jets were getting better. Season by season New York coach Weeb Ewbank was building up the club. He drafted a player here, traded for a player there. Of the original 1960 New York club (known then as the Titans), only three players were still on the team in '67: Bill Mathis, Don Maynard, and Larry Grantham.

In the Titan years the New Yorkers had played in the old Polo Grounds, a huge stadium that would soon be torn down. Sometimes there were fewer than 5,000 fans at a game. But that was hardly surprising. The game played by the Titans hardly resembled big league football.

In those days the players had problems on and off the field. By 1962 Titan owner Harry Wismer was even having trouble meeting the payroll. Grantham recalled just how bad things really were, "I was living at the

Concourse Plaza Hotel in the Bronx," he said. "I used
to cash my checks at a bank near there where I was
pretty well known. It was always the same story. 'We
can't give you immediate credit. We have to see if the
check will clear." Of course, a lot of times it wouldn't.
So I'd call Wismer or his secretary and they'd tell me,
'Oh, we've changed banks,' or something like that. I was
a young naive kid that didn't know any better and I
believed them."

By 1967 the New York team had clearly come a long
way. Now they played at new Shea Stadium, which was
filled each Sunday with 60,000 Jet enthusiasts who
believed in their team. Never mind the claims of the
NFL fans.

But in 1968 even their most faithful fans knew that
the Jets still had a long way to go. In part, Namath was
to blame. In his play selection, he was "pass happy." He
had so much confidence in his passing ability that he
often bucked the odds, throwing a football into a crowd
of receivers and defenders when it would have been
safer to try a ground play.

Namath was so good, of course, that many times even
his most daring passes worked. But when they didn't,
the other team would intercept and turn the game
around. And good as it was, Namath's passing game
just wasn't enough. Too often opposition defenses
stacked against the Namath pass, showing little respect
for the Jets' running game.

So, although Namath's statistics got more and more

impressive, the Jets' record was nothing to boast about. It made for grumbling among his teammates—and rightly so. For in failing to exert the kind of control required of a top quarterback, Namath was gaining a reputation at the expense of his team.

Of course, there was some justification for Namath's confidence in his air game. Not only did Joe have one of the strongest arms in the league—he also had some of the game's best receivers, the kind of men that made the pass a good bet. Wide receiver Don Maynard was uncanny in the way he caught a football. In a game where most men took shorter steps, Maynard moved with a long loping stride, and he ran patterns with what Namath jokingly referred to as "rounded corners." But no matter how unusual his style, Maynard did manage to get the ball.

Namath's other receiver, split end George Sauer, ran disciplined pass patterns. Where Maynard used speed to get by the secondary, Sauer relied on subtle feints, precise footwork, and crowd-pleasing acrobatics.

Joe also had the kind of protection a quarterback needs when he throws the ball. Jet backs Matt Snell and Emerson Boozer were strong and relentless blockers. Time after time they kept Namath out of the opposition's clutches.

But Snell and Boozer could run too. Snell, at 6-foot-2 and 219 pounds, was a crunching, straight-ahead runner. In contrast, Boozer had flair. At 5-foot-11 and 207 pounds, he was small by football standards—but he

Even Namath (12) can't get this pass off against Oakland's Carleton Oats.

bounced off tacklers like the ball in a pinball machine. His feet were covered with painful corns and bunions. But when Boozer carried the ball, he hurt the other team more than he hurt himself.

The third back, Mathis, was a capable replacement for either Snell or Boozer. He could run, block, and catch passes. And he had a knack for making the big plays under pressure.

The Jets had also provided Namath with great protection by assembling a dynamic offensive line. They could make either the run or the pass go, and they could hit. Right tackle Dave Herman, for instance, put more than his heart into blocking. He had a head too—size $7\frac{7}{8}$—which he used to full advantage. Herman did so much butting with his head that he actually went through two or three helmets a season.

Left tackle Winston Hill, on the other hand, claimed an artist's pride in his blocking. "I've made some blocks," he once said, "that were so beautiful that I wanted to frame them and hang them on the wall."

Herman and Hill had much to contribute on offense. But a stronger running game would also benefit the Jet defense. Its front four—Gerry Philbin, Paul Rochester, John Elliott and Verlon Biggs—was quick and aggressive. But the secondary was considered by many to be the weak link in New York's game. With better ball control, their load would be lightened.

The key cornerback was veteran Johnny Sample. He was a spirited player who could inspire the other defensive backs. But Sample was in his eleventh season as a pro, and some doubted that he was as good as he had once been. Certainly, he was still as controversial as ever.

During his long career, Sample had played in both leagues, and wherever he went—Baltimore, Pittsburgh, Washington, and finally New York—a furor was sure to follow. For John believed in intimidating pass catchers. "When they're trying to catch a football," he declared, "I'll break them in half if I have to." But physical punishment wasn't Sample's only weapon. He also used his own brand of psychological warfare. In his old NFL days, he once taunted Frank Gifford of the New York Giants so unmercifully that Gifford finally threw the football at him in frustration.

Those were the kinds of players Ewbank had assembled by '68. On offense and defense, New York was an all-around football team. If the Jets were ever to become the football power their followers were looking for, Namath would have to make the most of their talents. But could he do it?

The 1968 season's opener would be as good a test as any. Joe and the Jets were facing the Kansas City Chiefs, one of the strongest clubs in the league. The Jets got off to a good start, making the maximum use of all available talent. They blocked and they tackled. They moved the football on the ground and they moved it in the air. Time and again Namath hit Don Maynard on the broken pass patterns that were his specialty. When

New York cornerback Johnny Sample stops San Diego's Dick Post. The other Jet defenders are Biggs, Philbin, and Elliott (left to right).

Maynard changed a pattern, he would signal with upraised arm to Namath, and the quarterback would adjust. It worked just fine. In the first half Joe threw touchdowns of 57 and 30 yards to Maynard. New York also picked up a field goal for a 17–3 half-time lead.

But the tough Chiefs bounced back in the second half. With almost six minutes left in the game, New York was ahead by only one point 20–19. The Jets had the ball, but they were in a dangerous spot: on their own 5-yard line. If the Chiefs could get possession, they would be in easy scoring range. "There was no way in the world I thought the Jets could go from the 5-yard line and maintain possession until the end of the game," recalled Kansas City Coach Hank Stram.

But that's just what they did. Joe Willie mixed his plays beautifully. He used the run, he used the pass, and most important, he used the whole team. By the time the clock ran out, the Jets had run 15 plays and were still in possession of the football—not to mention the 20–19 victory. New York had passed its first test with flying colors.

Namath had beaten the clock against Kansas City by making the most of the men around him. And those men had responded. It was an impressive win. Perhaps this was the year the Jets would turn into a real team and not a one-man show. The New Yorkers would certainly give it a try.

A number of players grew beards, mustaches, and sideburns and vowed not to shave until they won the divisional title. A divisional title? Never before had the New York Jets taken themselves so seriously.

In that spirit New York took on the Boston Patriots. Namath did his part, of course, but again it was the team effort that got results. With the Jets leading 20–17, Mark Smolinski, a tough reserve playing on the Jet specialty teams, muscled through the Patriot line and pounced on a blocked punt.

Smolinski's play got the team going. On the final play of the drive Boozer careened off one tackler after another and somehow managed to stay on his feet for a touchdown. Later, tight end Pete Lammons caught a pass for another touchdown. Place-kicker Jim Turner iced it with his fourth field goal of the day, a 48-yarder. New York won its second contest, 47–31.

It was a promising start to the season. But New York teams had had their moments in the early autumn sun before. Unfortunately, when the weather got cold, so did the Jets. And while fans hoped that Namath had reformed, it would take more than two early-season glories to convince them. They knew Namath could still revert to his pass-happy ways and make havoc of a game.

And that's just what he did against Buffalo. When the Jets got off to a slow start, Namath refused to play the kind of game he had used so successfully in his last two outings. Instead, he became the old go-for-broke Joe. Again and again he put the football up for grabs. It was a desperate measure, and it cost him.

Halfback Emerson Boozer runs into a wall of Boston Patriots.

Buffalo's tough defensive backs, Booker Edgerson, Tom Janik, and Butch Byrd, knew what to do when a quarterback got too big for his football britches. They simply plucked the football out of the air and disappeared with it. Janik ran one interception back 100 yards for a touchdown. Edgerson and Byrd converted two other Namath passes into Buffalo touchdowns, helping the Bills to a 37–35 victory.

In one afternoon Namath had raised the ghost of sad Sundays past. Too many Jet games in previous seasons had been marked by a similar misuse of the pass. In games like those, Namath gave Jet fans the joe-willies. The two early wins began to look like flukes.

Even Joe's teammates wondered whether he had the one quality all great pro quarterbacks need—leadership. In the three years that Namath had been the AFL's premier attraction, his Jet teammates had pointedly ignored him when voting for the team's Most Valuable Player. They did not vote for their own quarterback.

Namath finally got the message. When New York went against the San Diego Chargers in the fourth game of the season, Joe Willie was a new man, using everything he—and the Jets—had to offer. Up front, Hill and Herman blocked with precision, while Boozer and Snell ran the football. And the defense did a tough and capable job. Even the secondary shone.

Johnny Sample was all over Lance Alworth, the Chargers' star pass catcher. And when he was not trying to bend Alworth out of shape, he was sassing him in a way that only Johnny could.

Namath? He used 40 running plays and 34 passing plays. It was the first time all season that he ran the ball more than he threw it. On pass plays, he avoided the dangerous patterns that had gotten him in trouble against Buffalo.

Nevertheless, with less than six minutes left in the game, the Chargers were leading 20–16. But instead of panicking, Namath shunned the use of the risky long pass in favor of shorter but surer throws. Starting from the New York 25, Namath methodically completed three of four passes to gain a first down on the Charger 40.

A crucial penalty moved the Jets to the San Diego 25. Here Smolinski, playing tight end in place of the injured Pete Lammons, caught a Namath pass for another first down at the 6. Then it was Boozer's turn. Three times Emerson carried the football. The third time he cracked through the San Diego line and into the end zone. New York had come from behind for a 23–20 win.

The next week against Denver, Joe learned again that he couldn't do it all by himself. Boozer was hurting, Snell and Mathis had bad knees, and Namath's blocking failed. The Jet machine broke down. Joe tried to pass anyway. But without protection he didn't have enough time to pass the ball. Rich Jackson, the Broncos' defensive end, got through time and again to pressure Namath. As a result, five of Joe's passes were stolen by a team that had intercepted none all season—

and the New Yorkers lost that game, 21–13.

Afterward, a remorseful Namath told newsmen, "I stink." Joe refused to put the blame elsewhere. Namath was finally facing up to his reponsibilities. If the Jets were to make it to the title, Joe Willie would have to lead them. Good times or bad.

If things looked bad in the San Diego game, they seemed even worse when Joe Willie went against Houston the next week. He was zero for 10 in his passing at one point, but the Jets stuck with him. As Ewbank put it, "He's the one who can get you there."

And Namath got them there in the end—with a little help from the team. Houston was leading 14–13 late in the game when the Jets began a drive from their own 20. This time it was Sauer who spurred the team. He caught three Namath passes in a row—twisting, diving, battling for the ball. Then Boozer caught Namath's fourth straight completion, a ball hurled at shoe-top level, and ran it to the Oiler 27.

Boozer kept his aching feet going. From the 27, he picked up two yards, and then he got 15 more. With two minutes remaining, the Jets had the ball just inside the Houston 10. Snell drove to the 2, and on the next play, scored a touchdown for a 20–14 Jet victory.

Namath had recovered from his shaky start by throwing 12 completions in 27 attempts for 145 yards. Moreover, he had suffered no interceptions and had used the running game wisely. Joe was learning. He had

The ball squirts away as Gerry Philbin tackles the Buffalo quarterback.

found that when his touch was off—and there were bound to be such afternoons—he had to stay cool and rely on his teammates.

In the next game, New York's second confrontation with Boston, Namath put into practice all he had learned. Following the opening kickoff, he led a precise 80-yard drive to a touchdown. First Boozer would hit into the line, spinning out like some crazy windup toy. Bang, bang. Boozer again and again. Then Namath would pass to Maynard or Sauer. And then Snell would churn through the middle of the Boston line, head lowered like an angry bull.

Run and pass. Namath used the combination expertly. By the fourth quarter, he had the Jets out in front 20–0. And he hadn't thrown a single interception. He left the game in the fourth quarter with a thumb injury and watched the Jets romp to a 48–14 victory.

Against Buffalo the next week, Namath's passing was off target. But this time he knew enough not to force things. Instead, he let his runners move the ball into field-goal range to keep the Jets in the game.

Then in the second half Joe took advantage of a Buffalo weakness. In their haste to cover Maynard and Sauer, the Buffalo pass defenders were leaving Pete Lammons free to the outside. From the Jets' 29, with New York trailing 21–19, Namath hit the open Lammons for a 25-yard gain. Joe went to him again on the next play. This time Lammons was interfered with as he tried to catch the ball, and the penalty put New York in field-goal range. Jim Turner's kick put the Jets in front 22–21. Later, Turner kicked another field goal for a 25–21 win.

It was the Jet kicker's sixth field goal of the day. He said it was the most he had kicked since an intrasquad game in Jersey City, New Jersey. "And I kicked for both teams that day," Turner said with a smile.

Meanwhile, Joe Willie was passing less and enjoying it more. Even on a so-so day, he kept control of the game. Against Buffalo he had completed only 10 of 28 passes, but he was intercepted only once by the Bills.

"There were times today when I threw the ball away intentionally," he said after the game. "In other years I had to try to force the pass. But now, with our defense, I can throw it away, take the field goal, and let the other team make mistakes against our defense."

The "pass happy" quarterback had come a long way. It was the fifth game in a row that Joe had failed to throw a touchdown pass. But Joe seemed to have developed a new sense of perspective. "This will be a win in the standings," he said. "No matter how we win it. It's the team that counts."

And the team was doing fine. After eight games New York led the Eastern Division with a 6–2 record. Second-place Houston was 4–5. Still, Jet teams had led their division before, only to fold at the end of the season.

In 1967, in fact, New York had lost the division title to Houston late in the season. The Oilers had clinched the Eastern title on a Saturday night in Miami. The next day, before a meaningless game against the San Diego Chargers, Jet president Sonny Werblin had received a telegram that read:

GOOD LUCK, SONY (*sic*), ON YOUR GAME WITH
THE CHARGERS. WE SAVED SECOND PLACE FOR YOU.
                    —THE HOUSTON OILERS

"Anybody hates to be downgraded," said Jet linebacker Larry Grantham, "and that's what they did with that wire."

Now as the Jets prepared for their second 1968 game with Houston, they remembered that telegram. In the cold, wet sludge of Shea Stadium the Jets went after the Oilers with a vengeance. They used a new formation to get their first touchdown. As usual, Sauer and Maynard, the two outside receivers, were stationed wide on opposite sides of the field. But this time, tight end Lammons split wide to the left rather than playing on the line, and halfback Boozer flanked to the right.

Thus, the Oilers were faced with four possible wide receivers. They had to use slower safety men to cover Sauer and Maynard, while the speedier Oiler cornerbacks went up against Lammons and Boozer.

Not surprisingly, Sauer and Maynard had no trouble getting open. Namath hit Maynard for 19 yards and Sauer for another 43 as the Jets moved to the Oiler 5. Two plays later, Mathis scored. New York went on to win 26–7. Houston sent no telegrams that day.

Next, New York faced the defending AFL champions, the Oakland Raiders. If the Jets won that game, they would be assured of at least a tie for the Eastern Division championship. The game was a wild one, filled with penalties and lots of scoring—and it ended in one of the strangest controversies in NFL history.

The game, scheduled to end at 7 P.M. Eastern time, was running late. As 7 o'clock approached, the Jets scored a field goal, going ahead 32–29 with 1:05 left to play. Then the National Broadcasting Company decided to cut off its television coverage of the football game to show the children's special, "Heidi," which was slated to start at seven. That decision deprived millions of people—especially Jet fans in New York—from watching an unbelievable finish.

While television viewers watched Heidi skipping through the Swiss Alps, the game continued. The Jets kicked off, and Oakland started at its 22-yard line. From there, Raider quarterback Daryle Lamonica threw to halfback Charley Smith for 20 yards. When a Jet illegally grabbed Smith's face mask, a penalty was called and Oakland got the ball at New York's 43. Lamonica then threw a 43-yard touchdown pass to Smith, giving Oakland a 36–32 lead.

Only 42 seconds remained, but the Jets still had time to score. They never got the chance, however. For Earl Christy was hit hard while returning Oakland's kickoff, and the ball squirted out of his hands toward the goal line. Oakland's Preston Ridlehuber scooped it up at the

2 and scored another Raider touchdown. That was all
for the Jets, who lost the game 43–32. Jet fans in New
York, who thought the Jets had won, were amazed to
hear later in the evening that they had lost—by eleven
points!

Would the Jets fall apart after the painful loss?
Namath made sure they didn't. Although he had gone
six games without a touchdown pass earlier in the
season, Joe Willie came through when the Jets needed
him most. Against San Diego the next week, he hit 17 of
31 passes for 337 yards and two touchdowns, leading
New York to a 37–15 victory. After the game, Charger
coach Sid Gillman said, "The way Namath threw today,
he could beat anybody."

But the Jets didn't have to beat anybody else to win
the Eastern Division. On Thanksgiving Day, Kansas
City eliminated the Houston Oilers from the divisional
race, and the title was all New York's. The Jets finished
the season with two more victories anyway, beating
Miami 25–17, and Cincinnati 31–7. Then they got ready
for the AFL Championship.

On December 29 at Shea Stadium the Jets again
faced the Oakland Raiders—but this time it was for the
league crown. The Raiders had won the league championship in 1967 and they were determined to repeat
that feat.

Always a rough and ready team, the Raiders seemed
to get especially fired up whenever they played against
the New Yorkers. With the all-important Super Bowl

berth at stake, the AFL championship game was sure to be an exciting—and hard-fought—battle.

But Joe and his Jets knew how to handle the Raiders now. They had learned what would work against Oakland in the "Heidi" game. Although the Raiders had finally edged out the Jets, Maynard had outfoxed rookie defensive back George Atkinson that whole afternoon. Namath decided to see if Maynard could repeat that performance.

And he did. Early in the game Maynard got by Atkinson four times. Twice Namath hit him with passes. The third time Atkinson was forced to interfere with the pass. Then Maynard scored the first points of the game on a 14-yard reception with a sharp break toward the sideline flag that left Atkinson stumbling. A 33-yard field goal by Turner gave the Jets a 10–0 lead at the end of the first quarter.

Meanwhile, Raider quarterback Daryle Lamonica was having trouble with the swirling Shea Stadium winds, which made his passes do funny things. But Lamonica finally caught on late in the first quarter when he got the Raiders moving on short passes to his running backs and longer ones to flanker Fred Biletnikoff. Early in the second quarter Biletnikoff scored on a 29-yard pass from Lamonica to make the score 10–7. Both teams then scored on field goals, so New York led 13–10 at the half.

In the third quarter the Jets' league-leading defense held fast. Once the Raiders moved all the way to the

New York 6-yard line, but in three plays they were unable to score the go-ahead touchdown. That marvelous line—Biggs, Philbin, Elliott, and Rochester—wouldn't budge. Oakland finally settled for a field goal that tied the score 13–13.

Then it was Namath's turn. In the bone-chilling cold he moved the New Yorkers. Here was Snell crashing up the middle; there was Boozer bouncing through the Raider defense. Joe and his Jets marched upfield.

It was a hard, violent game. Every time Snell or Boozer took the ball, they were met with great thudding force, the collision of pads making an eerie sound in the thin wintry air.

Namath was having his own troubles. Earlier he had dislocated a finger after being knocked down by an Oakland player. The Jets' team physician, Dr. James Nicholas, yanked the finger back to its proper shape and taped it to Namath's index finger. But the pain persisted. To make things worse, Joe's head was ringing from the blows that the Raider defense kept delivering.

But the teams were fighting for a championship. In times like this the name of the game was pain. Through it all, Namath kept the Jets moving. His offensive line—Hill, Herman, Randy Rasmussen, Bob Talamini, and John Schmitt—kept crashing through the Raider front wall. Then Boozer and Snell would speed through the holes, picking up valuable yardage a bit at a time.

In 13 plays the Jets went from their 20 to Oakland's 20. Then Namath stepped back and threw over two

Oakland defenders to Pete Lammons. Lammons caught the ball on the dead run for a touchdown.

Oakland was still fighting, however. Late in the third quarter, the Raiders had moved ahead 23–20 on a touchdown and a field goal. But then the Raiders kicked off to the Jets. From his own 32, Namath threw to Sauer who scrambled ten yards to the 42. Then Joe sent Maynard racing down the sideline. Maynard had expected to receive the ball over his left shoulder, but it was thrown to the other side. Seeing this, the Jet flanker twisted his body, reached out, and miraculously caught the ball before skidding out of bounds at the Oakland 6.

Now the Jets huddled. A whole season's effort was at stake. Namath called for a play in which he would roll out and look for a receiver. But as he tried to roll out on the snap, he saw Oakland linebacker Gus Otto hemming him in. Namath looked for Mathis, then for Sauer. Both were covered.

He turned, desperate, and there was Maynard cutting across the end zone. Joe threw a low pass. Maynard dived to his knees and caught it. The crowd went wild as the scoreboard lit up: New York 27, Oakland 23. The defense held, and when the clock ran out, the Jets were champions of the AFL. They had a quarterback for sure, but they had even more—a team!

And it was as a team that the New Yorkers came to the Super Bowl at Miami. By capturing the league crown, the Jets had proved themselves to the AFL fans. But there were still those who didn't think that counted

Maynard hangs on to the pass that won the game and the AFL championship.

for very much. Now the Jets faced the NFL champion Baltimore Colts.

Even their greatest supporters didn't think the upstart Jets had much of a chance there; but Namath brashly predicted victory—"guaranteed" it, as a matter of fact. Joe's boast made headlines all over the country. But it was really just his way of psyching himself up for the most important game of his career.

Of course, every Jet was doing the same thing in his own way. Johnny Sample watched films of the Colts until he was bleary-eyed. "I've been watching Willie Richardson [a Colt pass receiver] so much now that I feel I know him," he said.

Defensive back Randy Beverly was reading the papers and getting angry. "Some of the writers are making me out as the guy Baltimore's going to kill on the pass," he explained. "Well, I'm waiting to find out. Because I don't intend to play the clown for anybody."

The Colts' defensive line was said to be unstoppable. But the Jets thought otherwise. "I'm ready," said Dave Herman, vowing to stop Baltimore's monstrous defensive end Bubba Smith.

The other New York tackle, Winston Hill, was also ready. A radio man found that out the day several Jets came to his studio. The New Yorkers were to have their remarks taped after listening to previously recorded statements made by the Colts. "When the Colts' Ordell Braase came on," the radio man said, "I was watching Hill [who would be facing Braase], and his fists jerked shut and he sat up in his chair. He looked ready to take on Braase right then and there."

It was against Braase's side of the line that the Jet coaches had decided to run. That way the flow of plays would be away from the Colts great left linebacker, Mike Curtis. Curtis was a man to be avoided if at all possible.

It was a good decision—better than even coach Ewbank could have known. For Braase would be playing with a bad back. Baltimore hadn't let on that Braase was injured, but it didn't take long for the Jets to figure it out themselves.

"Nineteen straight" was the play. Namath gave the ball to Snell. Hill drove into Braase and heard him grunt in pain. Snell drove the Colt to the right, then cut to the left for a three-yard gain.

Back came Snell on the very same play. This time he gained nine yards plowing into Colt safety, Rick Volk. Volk had to be carried off the field.

And so it went. The Jets were "up." When the Colts called their blitz, sending their defensive backfield storming in to get Namath, Joe knew just how to handle it—he threw quick passes up the middle for big gains. Up and down the line the Jet blockers did their job. Even the great Bubba Smith was held in check.

When Baltimore had the ball, the Jet defensive line made the plays, assisted by linebackers Grantham, Atkinson, and Baker. And the secondary, still considered the weakest link in New York's defense, proved

Super-hero Matt Snell carries the ball in the Super Bowl.

otherwise. Beverly showed he was no clown by intercepting two passes, while Sample and Hudson got one apiece. And Billy Baird, who had been cut from the Colts years ago, got just what he wanted—sweet revenge. The little back knocked his former teammates all over the field.

In the end, though, it was "nineteen straight" and Snell. Snell, the unsung workhorse, finally had his day of glory. With Hill cutting Braase down like a sickle working through wheat, Snell ran all over the Colts. Don Shinnick, the Baltimore linebacker on the right side, saw little but the back of Snell's jersey for most of the afternoon.

Thirty times Snell carried the ball! When the afternoon was over he had gained 121 yards. Impressive statistics, but so were Namath's: 17 completions in 28 passes for 206 yards and no interceptions. But the most important numbers, of course, were 16–7. With that final winning score the New York Jets had become the first AFL team to win the Super Bowl.

Namath had called it—but the Jets had done it!

Baltimore Colts 1970

It was only the first game of the 1970 season, but the Baltimore Colts were already in trouble. Only two seasons ago, in 1968, they had won the National Football League championship and had been considered the strongest team in pro football.

But then disaster had struck. In January 1969 the Colts had become the first NFL team to lose a Super Bowl—to the upstart New York Jets. Then in the regular 1969 season, the Colts had fallen apart. Their 8–5–1 record had not even qualified them for the post-season playoffs, and the Baltimore fans, expecting a champion, had booed their former favorites.

Now against the unheralded San Diego Chargers in the 1970 opener, the Colts were trailing 14–13 with less

than a minute to go. They had the ball, however, and onto the field came a long-haired rookie named O'Brien. The program listed him this way:

O'Brien, Jim   WR   6–0   195   Cincinnati U.

He was a wide receiver (WR), but that was only part of the story. It was O'Brien's ability to boot field goals that made him really special. In pre-season training, O'Brien's kicks had been long and accurate. Even when the Colts ran "scream drills" in which defenders would rush him shouting the worst insults imaginable, O'Brien never wavered. He kicked the ball perfectly.

The Colts were extremely pleased with O'Brien on the field. But off the field it was another matter altogether. O'Brien was a kid who had strong ideas about "doing his own thing." He had started college at the Air Force Academy, but hadn't liked the way military life cramped his style. So he left and went to the University of Cincinnati where he could be himself.

The most obvious symbol of O'Brien's independence was his long shaggy hair. It was not the kind of hair style the Colts were used to, and most of them didn't like it one bit. They nicknamed the young rookie "Lassie" and teased him unmercifully.

But the Colt regulars didn't want to ride O'Brien too hard. Long hair or not, he promised to solve one of the Colts' biggest problems. Their veteran field goal kicker, Lou Michaels, had lost his touch in 1969, and that was one of the reasons the Colts had slipped. If they were to

Colt rookie Jim O'Brien: his hair was long but so were his kicks.

be winners in the NFL, where games were often decided by the margin of a field goal, they needed a toe like O'Brien's.

Now in the very first game of 1970, the rookie came off the bench in a clutch situation. The Colts were beginning play in the new American Football Conference of the NFL, competing mostly with old AFL teams. It was embarrassing for them to be trailing San Diego. Only O'Brien stood between them and defeat. Just as he had done in practice, he kicked the ball long and straight—through the uprights. The Colts won 16–14.

The next week the Colts faced the Kansas City Chiefs, winners of the Super Bowl in January 1970. It quickly became clear that the Colts still had plenty to worry about. The Chiefs scored 17 points in the first 16 minutes, and by halftime Baltimore trailed 31–6. It was a long evening, as the Colts finally lost 44–24.

After this humiliating defeat, sportswriters claimed again that Baltimore's glory years were over. They had lost the Super Bowl, they had followed with a mediocre season, and now in 1970, their performance did not seem promising.

Adding to their difficulties was a string of serious injuries. Tight end John Mackey, one of the all-time great ones, had a bad knee. His backup, Tom Mitchell, was also hurting. And so were running backs Jerry Hill and Terry Cole.

But the Colts' real problem seemed mental—not

physical. The loss of the Super Bowl had taken the swagger out of the Colts. When Baltimore had faced the Jets everyone (except Joe Namath) expected the Colts to run away with the title. The Colt defenders were thought of as supermen. Big Bubba Smith, the 6-foot-7, 280-pound defensive end, was said to discard blockers as if they were schoolboys. Mike Curtis, the linebacker, was known as "The Animal" because he was so ferocious. And so it went, right down the roster. But in one game the Jets had reduced the Colts to human dimensions.

In 1969 the Colts were no longer considered man-eaters. They were just another pro team. Defeat affected the Colts the way it did other clubs. It stung their pride and made them doubt themselves. It also made them doubt the man who had been their leader.

When Baltimore was riding high, it seemed that coach Don Shula could do no wrong. True, Shula had always been a rather strict disciplinarian. When the Colts were winning, his sharp words had seemed necessary to keep the players from becoming overconfident and careless. After their embarrassing Super Bowl performance, however, the Colts found their coach's criticism a lot more difficult to accept.

Shula was obviously a good coach, but he had lost his players' trust. When the Dolphins offered him the head coaching job at Miami before the 1970 season, he took it without a second thought. To replace Shula, the Colts hired Don McCafferty.

McCafferty was just what Baltimore needed—a relaxed coach with a quiet manner. Hopefully, he was the man who could get the Colts out of their troubled state. After the Chiefs walloped Baltimore, McCafferty encouraged his players instead of scolding them. Better days, he told them, were ahead. And he was right. In their next game, Baltimore defeated Boston 14–6.

Life in Baltimore was definitely looking brighter. McCafferty was coaxing the effort out of Baltimore that Shula couldn't. He became known as "Easy Rider" because of his low-key way. But the new coach wasn't the only positive force. Quarterback Unitas helped too. Even at the age of 37, Unitas still had an arm that was strong enough to turn a game around with one throw. And that's just what Johnny U. did in the Colts' next outing against Houston. In the last seconds of the game, he threw a 31-yard touchdown pass to wide receiver Roy Jefferson to beat the Oilers 24–20.

Slowly, the Colts were regaining the vim they'd had in the past. Baltimore was not the powerhouse it had been ten years earlier. But this '70 club had capable men, the kind of players it took to win a title.

Most of all, the Colts wanted to win. Remembering the Super Bowl defeat could demoralize a team, but given the right circumstances, the memory could motivate them instead. As linebacker Curtis said, "Going into that game, I continually heard, 'You've got to beat that longhair, that Joe Namath.' Yes, I thought, we've got to beat that longhair. But there was no dishonor in losing to the best—and that's what Namath was. Losing to the other Jets, dirty players like Johnny Sample, that was degrading."

Curtis was one of the Baltimore veterans McCafferty was relying on to spur a Colt comeback in 1970. And in the first four games of the season, Curtis made tackles with the pulverizing power that had marked his play in earlier years. So did defensive tackle Billy Ray Smith. Like Curtis, he had not forgotten the way the Jets had smeared the Colts' good name. In the locker room after that loss he'd said, "Money, marbles, or chocolate—I hate to lose."

Smith's words reflected the Colt feeling precisely. Since their big loss to the Jets, vindication was what the Colts wanted. But a real test lay ahead. For the Colts were about to come up against the Jets once again—this time in New York's Shea Stadium. It might be just another game for the Jets, but it had the importance of a crusade as far as the Colts were concerned. It was a chance to take at least some of the edge off Super Bowl III.

McCafferty got the team ready in his own fashion. No flaming pep talks or rah-rah locker room signs. That wasn't his way. But just before the team left for New York, McCafferty ran the film of the Super Bowl game—without a word. The film said it all. By the time Baltimore took the field, the players seemed more like tigers than colts.

Bam! On the first play of the game, Unitas threw to

Baltimore quarterback Johnny Unitas gets set to pass.

John Mackey on a sideline pattern, and big bad John ran through the New York secondary like a tank. When Mackey hit, the Jets toppled over like bowling pins. John barreled through for a 48-yard gain.

Mackey's run set up a field goal, which O'Brien converted for three points. That was just the start of things. The Baltimore defense was merciless, pounding super-Jets Emerson Boozer and Matt Snell into the ground. The Jet runners were hit from all directions, as the Smith boys (Bubba and Billy Ray) and Mike Curtis swarmed over the green-jerseyed Jets.

And on offense, old maestro Unitas was just as effective. Throwing to Eddie Hinton or Roy Jefferson on breakaway patterns or to Mackey for shorter yardage, Johnny U. showed he still had the magic touch. Mackey, who had started Baltimore rolling with his 48-yarder, was particularly dangerous. As one football man said later, "The thing I like about Mackey is the way he goes into a man when he's about to be tackled. He doesn't fold up. Instead he accelerates, and that means he's putting full pressure on the tackler rather than vice versa. That's the secret of most great power runners."

There was no secret about Baltimore's power that day. The Colts wanted to win—and win big. And that's just what they did. The next time they got the ball, they swept straight to the goal line. Unitas mixed his plays beautifully, running and passing the Colts downfield to a 10–0 lead.

The Colts were playing inspired football. They scored another quick touchdown, and in only six minutes they had put 17 points on the scoreboard. When the game ended, the Colts were in front 29–22. It didn't make up for the Super Bowl, of course, but it was a satisfying victory anyway.

McCafferty couldn't have been more pleased. But he reminded the team that it would take more of the same to bring the title back to Baltimore. A feeling was building among the Colts. Under the Easy Rider, maybe—just maybe—1970 would be their year.

McCafferty, was certainly doing his part. Said one Colt, "His manner is unique. He motivates you without making a lot of noise. He has a combination of quiet strength, a tremendous knowledge of football, and the determination to put it all together. Don Shula shouted a lot, but he didn't reach every single player. McCafferty does."

Another Colt added, "One night coach McCafferty came in to play poker with us. He sat in on one hand and won ninety-three dollars. Then he just took off. If you can still like a coach after that, he must have something special."

Now the Colts were once again pulling as a team. Setbacks that might have stopped them cold during their 1969 slump, were taken in stride this year. For example, when their top runner Tom Matte suffered a minor injury, the Colts had turned to a big rookie back, Norm (Boo) Bulaich. But Bulaich (the name rhymes with goulash) had his own troubles for a time. He was plagued by the old bugaboo of all runners—the fumble. The 6-foot-1, 218-pound rookie handled the ball as if it were a bar of soap.

After a few early-season fumbles, Bulaich tried to change his technique. To get a better hold on the football, he began carrying it with two hands. But that wasn't much of an improvement. Boo didn't lose the ball that way, but he lost the speed and body balance that had made him so impressive in training camp. Luckily, Bulaich got help from his teammates. They all encouraged him, especially Unitas. "Stop thinking about fumbling," Johnny urged, "and just run."

After Baltimore's next game against Boston, the Colts needed Bulaich more than ever. Tom Matte injured his knee in the first play of the game. The knee buckled, and Matte was finished for the season. But even without Matte, Johnny U. managed to get by Boston. Unitas, looking sharper each week, threw long and threw short. And he threw for touchdowns—to Jefferson, Jimmy Orr, and Jack Maitland.

On defense, coach Mac's boys were beginning to resemble the unit that had struck terror in the hearts of pro quarterbacks a few seasons before. Bubba and Billy Ray Smith, Fred Miller, and Billy Newsome up front, and Curtis, Ted Hendricks, and Ray May as linebackers were so fierce that Boston quarterback Joe Kapp was rushed into four interceptions. Boston fared no better on the ground, picking up only 45 yards for the whole afternoon. Meanwhile, the Colts picked up an easy 27–3 win.

The Colts looked even better the next week against Shula's rebuilt Miami team. Baltimore could do no wrong that day. The magic was everywhere. Punt returner Ron Gardin returned a kick 80 yards for a touchdown. Then Jim Duncan ran the second-half kickoff back 99 yards for another touchdown. The big Baltimore defense kept the Dolphins scoreless as Baltimore coasted to a 35–0 victory.

Baltimore kept rolling against Green Bay. And once again the defense led the way. The relentless Colt rush forced four interceptions. (That gave Baltimore a remarkable 17 interceptions in four consecutive games.) The Colts' secondary—Duncan, Rick Volk, Jerry Logan, and Charlie Stukes—was becoming more and more expert at catching other people's passes.

But to beat the Packers, it took cocksure kicker O'Brien. O'Brien's hair was longer than ever, but so were his kicks. The rookie had managed a 48-yarder against Boston earlier in the season. And now, under pressure, he booted two third-quarter field goals that made the difference in the game. By a score of 13–10 the Colts picked up their sixth straight victory.

It was no longer just the veterans that Baltimore relied on in the clutch. The kid kicker was just one of the new Colts who made a difference. Hendricks, Maitland, and Newsome did their part too. And running back Norm Bulaich had no more trouble

Miami tries to stop Jefferson, but the Colts gallop to a 35–0 win.

holding on to the ball. In fact, he gained 69 yards against the Packers.

Against Buffalo a week later, the Colts were held to a 17–17 tie. Bulaich, however, was a real winner in that game, carrying for 86 yards. That performance was good news to coach Mac, who had clearly found a replacement for the injured Matte.

With renewed confidence, Baltimore was looking more and more like the smooth-running team it had been back in '68. But the Colts could not afford to get overconfident, as they found out the next week. In a rematch between Baltimore and Miami, coach Shula's new team triumphed 34–17. It was a big loss for the Colts. In the Eastern Division of the American Conference, Baltimore was no shoo-in. The Dolphins were young, and getting better by the week. Miami was in striking distance of first place if Baltimore let up.

Even a so-so Chicago Bears team gave the Colts a good scare and proved they couldn't relax on any Sunday. The Bears managed to score 17 points before Baltimore got going. But then Unitas put the football up in the air—and the Colts back in the game.

Against the Bears, Unitas was in rare form. He completed 23 of 40 passes, many of them under pressure from the big Bear line. The aging quarterback looked like a kid again. In his high-topped black shoes, Unitas dropped into the pocket and let the ball fly. Again and again he hit Hinton, Jefferson, and big John Mackey.

Mack was back—and how. Perhaps he was not quite

as fast as he had been before his injury, but he was as determined as ever. And in the end, it was Mackey who made the difference. With Baltimore behind 20–14, Mackey hauled in a Unitas pass. He lugged it 54 yards for a fourth-quarter touchdown to give Baltimore a remarkable 21–20 come-from-behind victory.

Unitas was up against the natural elements when Baltimore played Philadelphia the following week. The 40-mile-an-hour winds that whistled through Baltimore's Memorial Stadium made the forward pass a risky business. But that didn't stop the Colts. First Jerry Logan scored on an interception. Then Charlie Stukes set up another Colt touchdown with a 47-yard interception return. Eddie Hinton added another TD on an end-around play. And Jim O'Brien defied the elements. On that wind-swept field the remarkable rookie kicked field goals of 45, 44, and 47 yards to help Baltimore to a 29–10 win.

Roy Jefferson had a big hand in the 20–14 Colt victory over Buffalo the following week. Jefferson had come to Baltimore just before the season started, in a trade with Pittsburgh. In '68 and '69 Jefferson had been the only NFL receiver to gain 1,000 yards. But he'd had too many conflicts with the Pittsburgh management, so the Steelers had unloaded him. No problems with coach Mac, though. Jefferson got on just fine at Baltimore. "Roy Jefferson," said McCafferty, "is one of the most gifted athletes I have seen. He has ballet-like moves."

Jefferson was not only smooth—he was also strong.

Big Bubba Smith tackles Buffalo quarterback Dennis Shaw.

"I'd heard a lot about 'bump and run' as played in the old American Football League," he said, "but it doesn't bother me. I'm as big [6-foot-2, 195] as most corner-backs—bigger than some—so bump and run isn't a big factor with me." Against Buffalo, Jefferson had his biggest day for the Colts, with five receptions for 125 yards.

The win in Buffalo's snowy War Memorial Stadium gave the Colts the Eastern Division AFC title. It also marked a return to glory for Colt teams. Not that the team had been away for long—only a season, in fact. But there were some football people who figured Baltimore, like Humpty Dumpty, couldn't be put back together again.

But Baltimore had done it—and in perfect irony their regular-season finale came against the New York Jets. Added to the coincidence was the reemergence of the Colts' forgotten man, reserve quarterback Earl Morrall.

Many had blamed Morrall for the Colt downfall in Super Bowl III—and not without some justification. Instant replays had shown that shortly before the first half ended, Morrall had failed to see Colt receiver Jimmy Orr in the clear. To be sure, the Colts had made more than one mistake that day. But to Baltimoreans, that play symbolized the Colts' ineptitude. In the hearts and minds of Baltimore fans, Morrall was best forgotten.

Of course, memories were short when it came to Morrall. For it was Earl who had replaced the injured

Unitas during the '68 season and taken the team through an incredible 13–1 season. Without Morrall, the Colts might never even have made it to the Super Bowl. Obviously he was not all bad.

Against the Jets in 1970, Morrall showed only his best. Entering the game late in the first quarter in place of Unitas, Morrall threw four TD passes, connecting twice to Hinton and once each to Orr and Ray Perkins. Morrall threw for 348 yards, as he led the Colts to a 35–20 win.

The victory made Baltimore 11–2–1 for the season, a record that did McCafferty proud. But the Easy Rider was not about to let the Colts rest on their laurels. "It's only a start," he told the team. "Make up your minds to that."

The Colts had had a good year, but it would take more than that to make up for Super Bowl III. Nothing less than the championship would do. But first the Colts would have to get through the AFC playoffs. The Cincinnati Bengals were the foe. Cincinnati coach Paul Brown had brought his Bengals a long way in a short time. An AFL expansion team in 1968, the Bengals had won their final seven games of the season to upset Cleveland for the AFC's Central Division crown.

Over 50,000 fans showed up at Baltimore's Memorial Stadium on the day after Christmas to see if the home team could snap the Bengals' winning streak. Unitas and company gave the Baltimore rooters what old St. Nick couldn't—one whale of a ball game.

On defense the Colts front four was in high gear. When Bubba Smith had starred at Michigan State, the fans would chant, "Kill, Bubba, Kill," to urge the big man on. But Bubba needed no rah-rah for this one. He was all over the Bengals, making tabby cats of them all. So was Billy Ray Smith, a veteran looking to go out a winner. Chocolate, money, or marbles, he still hated to lose. And the way he tackled the Cincinnati runners that day, Smith was bound to be a winner.

Baltimore's linebackers were just as strong. Mike "The Animal" Curtis hit with the ferocity that had earned him his knickname. The tag embarrassed him when he was in street clothes, but when Curtis put on his football uniform, the nickname seemed to fit. That day he hit and hit and hit some more. He even intercepted a pass.

Curtis wasn't the only one of the linebackers who made big plays. Cincinnati's lone scoring attempt—a 49-yard field-goal try by Horst Muhlmann—was blocked by Ray May.

Meantime, the Colt attack was clicking. Bulaich—the inept rookie earlier in the season—now played like a true pro. He ran through the Cincinnati line like a barrel rolling downhill. There was just no stopping him. Boo was on his game that day, gaining 116 yards on 25 carries.

On that cold and windy day, Unitas showed that he was still a big-play quarterback, throwing touchdown passes of 45 yards to Jefferson and 53 yards to Hinton.

O'Brien's field goal was hardly necessary as Baltimore picked up an easy 17–0 win.

The Colts were on their way. But it was the Oakland Raiders the Colts would have to beat for the AFC title—and another shot at the Super Bowl. And the Raiders were not the pushovers that the Bengals had been. For years the Raiders had been one of football's toughest teams. A game against Oakland was truly a battle. When people like Ben Davidson and Ike Lassiter came for a quarterback, it was not just to sack him; it was to "ring bells." When the Raiders hit, they hurt.

The Raiders never let up on offense either. Up front to block were Gene Upshaw and the man known as Double Zero—center Jim Otto. They made the holes that 6-foot-1, 230-pound Hewritt Dixon barreled through.

Oakland's passing attack was just as tough. Quarterback Daryle Lamonica was always a long-ball threat. Lamonica, sometimes called the Mad Bomber, liked to throw the ball for distance. And receiver Fred Biletnikoff was the perfect guy to catch it. Biletnikoff was as clever as any pro at running patterns to get free.

But Baltimore was not a team to be intimidated. Johnny U. was a master at mixing the plays, and that's what he did against Oakland. The old pro neutralized the Raider's monster-sized defense with a cunning selection of run and pass. First he'd send the rookie, Bulaich, into the line. Norm swept through like a hurricane, knocking down those vaunted Raiders.

Norm Bulaich (36) scores against Oakland in the AFC title game.

Then Unitas retreated into the pocket set up by his linemen—blockers like Bob Vogel, Glenn Ressler, and Bill Curry—and he threw the ball. Hinton, Perkins, Jefferson, Mackey—he hit them all, working well against Oakland's top-notch defensive secondary. Unitas was on his game—no question about it. He moved the Colts deep into Oakland territory, where O'Brien kicked a 16-yard field goal to give Baltimore a 3–0 first-quarter lead. And in the second quarter he led the team on another drive, snapping passes through the winter chill as he had been doing for more than a decade.

Meantime, the Colt defense was doing its job. Bubba and Billy Ray Smith and Curtis gave the 56,368 fans plenty to shout at. When big Dixon lugged the football, he got considerable attention from Baltimore. Usually he got caught in a traffic jam around the line of scrimmage.

Lamonica couldn't cut loose either. The Colt rush was so fierce, he never got enough time to throw his famous bombs. The Colt defense did not allow Oakland to score until late in the first half—and even then all Oakland could manage was a field goal by George Blanda. At the half Baltimore led 10–3.

Baltimore was playing well, but the Raiders weren't out of the game yet. In the third quarter Blanda (replacing Lamonica, who had been injured in the second quarter), threw to Biletnikoff for 38 yards and a touchdown to tie the game at 10–10.

Baltimore quickly responded, turning to Bulaich to get things going. And Boo ripped through the Raider line like a demon, bouncing off Raiders and speeding on. He showed the Raiders that pain was a two-way game. Bulaich hit, and Bulaich hurt. He made the Oakland line dig in.

And then Unitas let the ball fly. Bing, bang! Once more the Colts drove into Raider territory. And when the attack finally stalled, there was another rookie to the rescue. Sure-footed O'Brien came onto the field and kicked the ball 23 yards through the goal posts.

That wasn't the end of it either. On Baltimore's next drive Bulaich—on his way to a 71-yard performance for the day—got tough when it counted. Eleven yards away from the goal line, he took the ball and didn't stop until he was in the end zone.

But the play that finished Oakland was one with a special formation rigged up by McCafferty—a tight T with Jefferson, normally a receiver, at the fullback slot. Out of that alignment, Ray Perkins eluded the Raider defense, caught Unitas' pass and ran it 68 yards for the touchdown. And that was it. The final score: Baltimore 27, Oakland 17.

The Colts were back where they belonged: on top. Baltimore was the champion of the American Football Conference. It was a fine turnaround from the season before. But as McCafferty reminded the Colts, it was not the end of the line. From Bubba to Billy Ray to Unitas, the Colts knew what coach Mac meant. There was only one way to cap the season, and that was by winning the game that had undone the Colts to begin with—the Super Bowl. Only a win in pro football's big game would reestablish Colt glory.

With that in mind, Baltimore got ready. The game was set for the Orange Bowl in Miami. This time the foe was Dallas, a team rich in football talent. At every position the Dallas Cowboys were strong. Their star-studded roster included names like Bob Hayes, Bob Lilly, Duane Thomas, George Andrie, Chuck Howley, and Ralph Neely. On offense and defense the Cowboys were loaded. For most of the season Dallas had been red-hot. After a stunning mid-season 38–0 loss to the St. Louis Cardinals, the Cowboys had won their last seven games.

But Baltimore had waited a long time for this one. The Colts were wound up. And so, it turned out, were the Cowboys. Both teams were so eager to win the championship that they made mistakes. In fact, they made so many mistakes that for years after, Super Bowl V was known as the Blooper Bowl.

That didn't mean the teams coasted. On the contrary, the hitting was hard. And the game was exciting. It was also a bit bizarre. For with Baltimore trailing 6–0 in the second quarter, Unitas threw a pass to Eddie Hinton, who reached up and touched the ball. It skidded off his hands and then off Cowboy Mel Renfro's—and right into the arms of John Mackey. Big John gathered it in and ran to daylight—a 75-yard touchdown. But then

O'Brien's try for the extra point was blocked—another unusual sight.

More surprising turns were ahead. For later in the second half, Dallas defensive end, Andrie, came steaming through the Colt line to send Unitas sprawling. That blow did something that few teams had accomplished in all season—it stopped Johnny U. But it didn't stop the Colts.

For Baltimore had Earl Morrall in reserve. Morrall, of course, was the man many blamed for the Super Bowl III fiasco. And now here he was again with a second chance. But as the clock ticked away, Morrall seemed unable to take advantage of it. By the end of the third quarter Baltimore was behind 13–6.

But the Colts weren't finished yet. Midway through the final period, Baltimore safety Rick Volk intercepted Dallas quarterback Craig Morton's pass on the Cowboy 33 and ran it to the 3 before being tackled. Two plays later, Colt running back Tom Nowatzke scored. This time O'Brien's point-after-touchdown was good. The game was tied 13–13.

The game appeared to be heading for a sudden-death overtime. Dallas was back in its own territory and going nowhere, but time was rapidly running out. On third and long yardage, Dallas quarterback Craig Morton threw in desperation to Dan Reeves. The ball bounced off Reeves' fingers and into the hands of Mike Curtis, who ran the ball back to the Dallas 28.

It was here that Earl Morrall's long experience paid

off. There was scarcely a minute left, and he knew that he should run it down to a few seconds before leaving the ball for the field-goal kicker, Jim O'Brien. Morrall called two running plays, waited until the clock showed only nine seconds, then called time out.

Now the whole season rested on the shoulders of long-haired Jim O'Brien. He was kicking from the 32-yard-line for the Super Bowl victory. As the team lined up, the Cowboy defenders began screaming insults and threats—it was no drill this time. The ball was snapped, and O'Brien kicked . . .

The bottom line of the scoring summary told the story:

4th Qtr.   14:55   FG   O'Brien   32 yards

"Lassie" had done it and so had the Colts, winning 16–13. Baltimore was back.

Dallas
Cowboys
1971

In Hollywood Westerns the cowboys were always the good guys—and the good guys always won. But it wasn't that simple in Dallas, Texas. The Dallas Cowboy football team could win all season, getting into championship playoffs year after year. But when the chips were down and the big money was at stake, the Cowboys always lost, and some other team rode off into the sunset.

As the 1971 season began, the Cowboys could look back over five years of frustration. It all started in 1966 in the NFL championship game against the Green Bay Packers. Dallas had the ball inside the Packer 10-yard line as the final seconds ticked off the clock. But the Cowboys couldn't score the touchdown that would have

tied the game and sent it into overtime.

In 1967 Green Bay snatched the championship from the Cowboys again. This time in weather so cold that several players were treated for frostbite, Dallas was leading with only seconds to go. But the Packers had the ball on the one-yard line. The Cowboy defense held for three plays, but on fourth down Packer quarterback Bart Starr scored the touchdown to give the Pack a 21–17 win.

In 1968 and '69 the Cleveland Browns derailed the Cowboy express in the playoffs, upsetting strongly favored Dallas teams 32–20 and 38–14. In the last game the Dallas fans were so frustrated that they booed the team off the field.

Then in 1970 the Cowboys made it all the way to the Super Bowl. But their reputation for losing the big ones grew even worse. This time they lost to the Baltimore Colts when the Colts' Jim O'Brien kicked the winning field goal with five seconds to play.

It was not for lack of talent that Dallas lost the big games. Dallas had a computerized scouting system that kept turning up top-flight football players. To run the ball, the Cowboys had Calvin Hill, Duane Thomas, and Walt Garrison. To catch it, they had Lance Alworth, Mike Ditka, and Olympic sprint champion Bob Hayes. They had fine blockers and tacklers. And they had a coach, Tom Landry, whose football mind was as keen as any in the game.

In his playing days as a defensive back for the New York Giants, Landry was already a smart football man. He wasn't big or exceptionally fast but if he couldn't outrun opposing players he could often outthink them. By carefully studying the teams he faced, Landry usually managed to be in the right place at the right time.

As a coach, Landry devised a coordinated system of defense where players responded to certain "keys" in the offense. It was not simply the head-knocking straight-ahead defense used by other pro teams. Nor was the Dallas offense the simply constructed one that Lombardi favored at Green Bay. Dallas' system was far more intricate. Each Dallas player had a specific task on every play. And when everyone did his job properly, the play worked. "We run a multiple offense and must take advantage of situations as they present themselves," Landry said.

The Cowboys won a lot of games with Landry's system. But there was an almost robot-like quality to their play. As former Cowboy Pete Gent once put it, "Landry's system of football is directed in the hope of finally ending up with eleven complete strangers making up the team, each person knowing his job and the system completely, and interacting with his teammates only as specified in the playbook."

Landry's style did not encourage the team spirit that players developed in a less complicated system. And, according to pro football men, it was team spirit that Landry's clubs lacked. In a key game, that spark often made the difference between victory and defeat.

But Landry, a religious man, had the patience of Job, the long-suffering biblical figure. The thinking man's coach had great confidence in his system, and he stuck to his X's and O's. But there was one thing Landry wasn't so sure about. The coach was in a muddle about a quarterback. Dallas had two quarterbacks—Craig Morton and Roger Staubach—and Landry couldn't decide who he wanted to run the Cowboy offense.

Morton was the man Landry had used in past seasons. At 6-foot-4 and 214 pounds, Morton had good size for the position. But Morton couldn't seem to give the Cowboys the spark they so badly needed. Even Morton realized that something was missing. The season before, he had even undergone hypnosis to get "up" for the games. Physically, Morton wasn't in perfect shape either. He'd had arm trouble in 1970, and the injury appeared to be a lingering one. Still, Morton operated in the conservative style the coach practiced, and he remained a favorite with Landry.

Staubach, on the other hand, was a bold quarterback. When Roger faded back to pass he might change his mind and run with the ball. Staubach ran like a prairie rabbit, and he had an uncanny instinct for slipping tackles.

At the Naval Academy, where he had played in college, his slipping, sliding style had earned him the

Coach Landry's dilemma: the scrambling Staubach (12) or steady Morton?

name of Roger the Dodger. It had also gained him the Heisman Trophy in his junior year. But in the pros it earned him only grudging respect from Landry. Exciting as it was, Roger's scrambling ran against the coach's grain. Staubach had spent his first three years with the Cowboys trying to convince Landry that he was the man to win the big one for Dallas.

Landry used men like gridiron chess pieces. And in that sort of scheme the flashy Staubach was clearly not an easy fit. But it was just as clear that Morton was no dynamo at the position. Morton or Staubach? For Landry it was still a puzzle as the '71 season began. Landry finally came up with a surprising solution. He decided to try a platoon system. He would use both quarterbacks, alternating them in separate but equal pieces of action.

It was a plan that had not been used successfully since 1951 when the Los Angeles Rams had won a championship using both Bob Waterfield and Norm Van Brocklin at quarterback. Over the years split occupancy of the quarterback position had come to be thought of as bad strategy. Each quarterback gives a team a special rhythm, a unique tone. It would be difficult for any team to do a Sunday afternoon's work to two different beats.

Dallas learned that lesson early in the '71 season. With two quarterbacks, Dallas was not the team it had been in years past. Although they usually let down in the clutch, the Cowboys had always compiled top records in regular-season play. But now the Cowboys couldn't even win the games on the schedule—not the way they had before.

There was no apparent decline in the skills of the players. Bob Hayes could run and fetch a football as fast as any man in the game. Lance Alworth could still catch them with the acrobatic twists that had made the little guy such a favorite with crowds. And Hill, Thomas, and Walt Garrison made as much yardage running the football as ever.

The Cowboys were just as impressive on defense. The front line was particularly awesome. Known as the Doomsday Four, it included George Andrie, Bob Lilly, Jethro Pugh, and Larry Cole. They did to runners what Zorba did to grapes—stomped them! In five of Dallas' first seven games the front line held their opposition to 100 yards rushing. And all that time the Cowboy offense was gaining big total yardage—rarely under 300 yards a game.

Dallas was right up there in the league's statistical standings, except where it counted most—in the won–lost column. Despite their fine play, the Cowboys were losing almost as many games as they won. In the early part of 1971 it went like this:

Cowboys 49	Bills 37
Cowboys 42	Eagles 7
Redskins 20	Cowboys 16
Cowboys 20	Giants 13
Saints 24	Cowboys 14
Cowboys 44	Patriots 21
Bears 23	Cowboys 19

Midway through the season Dallas was 4–3, two games behind the Washington Redskins in the Eastern Division. Obviously, the two-quarterback system wasn't working.

Some people claimed the missing ingredient was simply "heart." According to their theory, the toll of big games lost had finally gotten to the Cowboys, who no longer thought they could win when it counted. Dallas, they believed, had finally given up the fight.

But Tom Landry had strong beliefs of his own. In his office was a signed portrait of Billy Graham, the evangelist. And Landry took it for gospel that Dallas was not finished. As the coach liked to say, "The Apostle Paul says suffering brings on endurance, endurance brings character, and character brings hope."

And Landry still had one hope. That hope was the 6-foot-3, 197-pound Staubach. Even Landry had to admit that Roger the Dodger knew how to make a team move. And if the Cowboys were going to make their move for the championship, they would have to do it soon. Any more losses at this point in the season would be disastrous to the team's morale.

Staubach got a chance to show what he could do in Dallas' next game against the St. Louis Cardinals. And for a while he couldn't seem to do very much at all. St. Louis was leading 10–6 in the third quarter when Jim Hart threw a pass to St. Louis end Jackie Smith for an apparent touchdown. But Cardinal rookie tackle Dan Dierdorf was caught on a holding penalty, and the touchdown was nullified.

Then Staubach went to work. He began throwing to Lance Alworth. With remarkable grace, the acrobatic Alworth raced downfield, leapt into the air to grab the ball, and kept on going. Alworth was so fast and smooth that at San Diego, where he had played before coming to Dallas, his teammates called him Bambi.

Against St. Louis, the fleet-footed Alworth lived up to that nickname, catching one pass after another. And when Alworth wasn't running with the ball, Staubach himself was scrambling for yardage. The Cowboys began to move. When he had the Cardinals pass-conscious, Staubach handed the ball to Duane Thomas.

After a preseason contract squabble with the Cowboys, Thomas had blasted Dallas management—from the general manager on down. He had even criticized Landry, referring to the unemotional coach as "Plastic Man." But on the field, Thomas held no grudges. Against St. Louis he gave his all. In the easy gliding way that reminded football people of the great Jim Brown, Thomas ran the football. Mostly he went wide, turning his speed up an extra gear to elude the Cardinal tacklers.

The Dallas drive continued. Getting yeoman service from the blocking linemen, the Cowboys moved all the way to the 4. From there Staubach passed for the touchdown to tight end Mike Ditka, putting Dallas ahead 13–10.

But the game wasn't over yet. The Cardinals bounced

Staubach passes over the outstretched arms of St. Louis' Rolf Krueger.

back with a field goal to tie the score 13–13. With time running out, the Cowboys began another drive. And again it was to Alworth that Staubach threw. Alworth bounced off the field like a trampolinist. Three times he caught the ball in heavy traffic. The last catch put the ball deep in Cardinal territory. But then the Dallas drive stalled, and they were faced with a fourth down on the Cardinal 19-yard line with 1:43 left to play.

Into the contest came stocky (5-foot-7, 185-pound) Toni Fritsch. Fritsch had come from Austria to Dallas when Cowboy general manager Tex Schramm decided the team needed a good soccer-style place-kicker. No wonder: most of the leading field-goal kickers in the pros were now booting them that way. In Austria, Fritsch had been a hero on the country's national soccer team.

Now, as he lined up the kick, Cardinal linebacker Larry Stallings began taunting Fritsch. "You're gonna miss it!" he screamed, trying to unnerve Fritsch. Stallings could have saved his breath, because Fritsch hardly understood English. The Austrian calmly kicked a 26-yard field goal to win the game for Dallas 16–13.

It was a big win for the Cowboys. With Roger Staubach as full-time quarterback, Dallas had come from behind for the victory. And that same day, Washington had been tied by Philadelphia, so the Cowboys gained in the conference race. But they still had a long way to go if they wanted to get rid of their "loser" label.

The next week it was the Cowboys' turn to play Philadelphia. This time Dallas' defense stole the show. The Cowboy front wall put on the pressure. When the Eagle backs tried to run with the ball, they went nowhere—thanks to Cowboy defender Jethro Pugh. Pugh suffered from ulcers, an ailment brought on by worrying. But this time it was the Eagles who had to worry.

The other Dallas hero was Bob Lilly, who could "make bells ring" in a man's head when he tackled him. Lilly was 6-foot-5 and 260 pounds, with much of his bulk in the shoulders and arms. Even teammates who played against him in scrimmages were awed by his strength. "He's like a boxer hitting you from six inches," explained Dan Reeves. "He doesn't have to get a running start to hurt you."

Lilly had more than might going for him. He was amazingly quick and agile and seemed to sense what the opposing blocker wanted to do on the play. More often than not, Lilly made sure the blocker was frustrated. "I didn't know what hands were till I played across from Lilly," said offensive lineman Jake Kupp. "When I set to block him the first thing he does is grab my shoulder with those big sensitive hands. When he feels me commit myself to either the inside or the outside, he'll throw me off balance. I think it's mostly reaction. I doubt if he has a predetermined plan most of the time."

Lilly and company held the Eagles to a mere 44 yards

rushing. Meantime, Staubach was having an easy time against the Philadelphia defense. He threw 14 completions in 28 tries for 176 yards. But passing was only part of his contribution that day. The artful dodger slipped away from onrushing linemen with such success that he ended up as Dallas' leading ground gainer, with 90 yards for the afternoon. More important, he led the Cowboys to a 20–7 victory.

It was another big win, for that afternoon the Redskins had lost to the Chicago Bears. But the Cowboys were still half a game out of first place. The Redskins were the Cowboys' next opponents, and if they could beat Dallas now, the Skins would be tough to catch as the season wound down to the finish.

But the Cowboys were determined to be winners for a change. Right from the start Dallas took charge. The bone-rattling defense came down hard on Washington backs Charley Harraway and Larry Brown. All afternoon those two bounced like rubber balls off the Doomsday Four. When they did manage to slip by, Dallas linebackers Dave Edwards, Lee Roy Jordan, and Chuck Howley made sure they didn't get far.

But the Redskin defense was nearly as tough. Made up of aging veterans (they were known as "The Over the Hill Gang"), the Washington team had enormous pride—as well as enormous power. This was a unit that spoiled for a fight.

But Staubach gave the Redskin defense just a bit

more than it had bargained for. When Washington applied the pressure, Roger the Dodger responded. He threw to Hayes, Alworth, Ditka, and reserve tight end Billy Truax. Occasionally, he hit running backs Garrison and Reeves too. Every time Washington put the squeeze on, Staubach slithered away. The Redskins kept coming on strong, but Roger broke free from onrushing Redskins five times—gaining a total of 49 yards, 26 of them on the game's only touchdown. The contest ended with Dallas ahead 13–0.

If Dallas was indeed a machine, then all its parts were running perfectly that day. The Cowboys had gotten the big effort in every department. The defensive secondary—Mel Renfro, Herb Adderley, Cliff Harris, Cornell Green, and Charlie Waters—was particularly outstanding. Washington quarterbacks Billy Kilmer and Sonny Jurgensen were simply unable to find receivers in crucial passing situations because the Dallas safeties had completely cut off the airlanes.

Cowboy kicker Mike Clark was another standout. Early in the year Clark had lost his job to Toni Fritsch when he repeatedly missed field goals at short range. But then Fritsch was injured, and Clark got another chance. He made the most of it against the Redskins, kicking field goals of 26 and 48 yards.

It was indicative of the kind of depth Dallas had always had. The Cowboys' reserves were so good they might have been starters on another team. Calvin Hill and Dan Reeves at the running backs, Gloster

Dallas defenders Pugh and Cole rush Redskin Larry Brown.

Richardson at wide receiver, Billy Truax at tight end, and Craig Morton at quarterback could all be counted on when they were needed.

Against the Rams the following week it was another reserve, kick-returner Isaac Thomas, who got things going for Dallas. Thomas took the opening kickoff 89 yards for a touchdown. Then Staubach went to work.

In the second quarter Staubach sent Bob Hayes on a long pass pattern. He picked the right man to run it. Hayes had been an Olympic gold medal winner for the United States in the 100-yard dash, and shared the record for that distance at 9.1 seconds.

Fast as he was, Hayes had not always seemed a natural as a pass receiver. There was some question as to whether he had the hands for the game. Hayes' hands were small and sensitive. In a college all-star game a quarterback named Craig Morton had thrown passes into Hayes' hands and cracked the skin between the fingers. Other times Hayes just dropped the ball. Said one football scout: "Hayes has 9.1 speed and 12-flat hands."

But Hayes didn't have any trouble against the Rams. When Staubach threw the ball out there, Hayes gathered it in as smooth as a magician's plucking flowers out of the air. And then he ran with the hard-driving strides that made him a world champion sprinter. There was no catching him as he raced 51 yards to a touchdown. Later in the game, Staubach threw to Alworth for a

21-yard score, and then Duane Thomas drove over the goal line from five yards out to give Dallas the 28–21 victory.

The Cowboys were riding high, making the most of the other teams' mistakes. And they made very few mistakes on their own. In the final weeks of regular-season play, Dallas looked like the power it was supposed to be. The Cowboys finished the season with three easy routs, beating the Jets 52–10, the Giants 42–14, and the Cardinals 31–12.

But, of course, with Dallas it all meant nothing if the team failed in the big playoff games. Unless the Cowboys could win the championship they would still be known as losers.

First the Cowboys would have to win their NFC divisional playoffs. Dallas, as the best team in the Eastern Division would meet the Central Division champs, the Minnesota Vikings. Minnesota was a hard, defense-oriented team. The Vikings' front four were as tough as any in the league. Known as the Purple People Eaters, Carl Eller, Jim Marshall, Alan Page, and Gary Larsen gave Minnesota an impressive front line.

But the Cowboy defense could be just as impressive, as the Vikings found out right away. The first time Minnesota got the football, Cowboy Larry Cole cracked Viking ball-carrier Dave Osborn so hard that he fumbled. Then it was the Dallas offense's turn to shine.

Staubach sent the speedy Hayes downfield against

Duane Thomas goes over and around the Viking defense in the NFL playoffs.

the Vikings' Ed Sharockman. Guarding against being "burned"—the pros term for being scored against on a pass—Sharockman gave ground. Too much ground. Hayes put the brakes on, turned, and caught Staubach's pass. With the ball in field-goal range, Clark proceeded to kick it 26 yards for a 3–0 Cowboy lead.

In the second quarter the Dallas defense stopped the Vikings again. This time Chuck Howley intercepted a pass thrown by Viking quarterback Bob Lee, and ran it back to the Minnesota 37. The Cowboys couldn't carry the ball in for a touchdown, but Clark kicked another field goal. Dallas 6, Minnesota 0.

And so it went. Against the powerful Dallas defense, the Vikings were unable to hold on to the ball. Four interceptions and one fumble turned the ball over to Dallas again and again. Staubach made the most of the situation, triggering the attack by completing 10 of 14 passes for 99 yards and a touchdown.

And when Staubach wasn't throwing the ball, he was handing it off to running back, Duane Thomas. Thomas, still unhappy with his salary settlement, was now virtually silent off the field. On airplanes Thomas would sprawl in his seat, silent as a sphinx. He wouldn't even reply to the stewardesses when they asked him what he wanted to eat. His teammates weren't too disturbed by his behavior because when he was on the field, Thomas' actions spoke louder than words. Against the Vikings, he carried 21 times for 66 yards and a touchdown to help Dallas win 20–12.

It was a mere beginning. Dallas was not ready to celebrate yet. Not with its history. Instead, Cowboy thoughts ran to their next game. Dallas still had to beat San Francisco for the NFC title—and a berth in the Super Bowl. If the Cowboys blew this one, they would go from champs to chumps in one day.

It was obvious from the pregame tension in the dressing room that was not just any game. The team's good name was on the line, and the Cowboys knew it. Even the mild-mannered Landry showed it in the tight draw of his mouth.

All that tension exploded as soon as the Cowboys hit the field. Lilly led the defensive play, tearing into the 49er backfield as if he had called the plays himself. On the snap of the ball, the Cowboys came on like wild warriors, busting up everything in their path. Up and down the line the Dallas defense moved with astonishing speed.

Soon San Francisco quarterback John Brodie tried to slow the fierce rush by calling for a screen pass. In the screen pass, the offensive linemen fake a block, then let the defense pour into the backfield. The quarterback retreats quickly in pretended panic. But at the same time, blockers are setting up a wedge in front of a back. The back takes a short pass from the quarterback and races downfield, protected by his blockers. If all goes well, the defense is out of position and the play goes for a long gain.

Bob Lilly drops 49er quarterback John Brodie in the NFC championship.

But the Dallas linemen were not just tough—they were smart too. When Brodie threw to his back, Cowboy lineman George Andrie was right there to catch the ball. Andrie lugged it all the way to the San Francisco 2. Then Calvin Hill banged in for the touchdown: Dallas 7, San Francisco 0.

The Dallas defense continued to work on Brodie. Landry and assistant coach Ernie Stautner had noticed in game films that Brodie's passing motion was not entirely overhand. Therefore, if the Dallas defense rushed him with hands up high, they could deflect the ball. And that's just what they did. Before long, Dallas had possession again.

The Cowboys were just as effective on offense. After running back Calvin Hill limped off the field with an injury, Walt Garrison came in. With the pressure on, Staubach gave the ball to the reserve. That suited Garrison just fine. He liked being in the thick of action. Garrison was a Cowboy in more ways than one. When he wasn't carrying the ball up the middle for Dallas, he could often be found swinging out of a chute on a Brahma bull as an off-season rodeo cowboy.

Garrison enjoyed putting his physical well-being on the line, and now he did it with relish. He got the ball, thudded into 49er tacklers, then spun away, finding little alleys to power his way through. Garrison made no long gains but he made four yards, then seven and then three and two, legs always churning for another inch of precious ground. Garrison got the ball all the way to the 3. Then Duane Thomas scored the touchdown. And that was it: Dallas 14, San Francisco 3. On to the Super Bowl.

With high hopes, the Cowboys prepared to meet the American Football Conference's Miami Dolphins. Seasons had come undone for Dallas teams, but its men had not. They had stuck it out in a year when it would have been easy to give up. That resolve had gotten them to the Super Bowl. Still, in pro football the Cowboys were a bust, their history full of missed chances. Now they had a chance, maybe their last chance, to put things right. And this time the Cowboys appeared ready to take it.

Right from the start Dallas forced the breaks. Six minutes into the action, Miami's fullback, Larry Csonka, was hit hard and fumbled. The Cowboys' Chuck Howley recovered the ball, and Dallas moved downfield. Again Garrison made the big yards rushing —on plays up the middle for eight to ten yards. Then Staubach hit Hayes for 21 yards. And from there Clark kicked a field goal. The Cowboys were on their way.

This time there was no stopping them. From start to finish they played with an abandon they had never shown before. On offense, Duane Thomas and Garrison burst into the Dolphin line and tore away from tacklers. Often they didn't have to do even that. On this day the offensive line—Dave Manders, John Niland, Tony

Walt Garrison picks up some big yards against Miami in the Super Bowl.

Liscio, Blaine Nye and Rayfield Wright—opened up holes big enough for a freight train to roar through.

Their blocking was just as effective for Staubach when he chose to pass. He threw 12 completions in 19 passes for 119 yards and two touchdowns as Dallas coasted to a 24–3 victory.

"When I'm the quarterback," Staubach once said, "and I walk on the field, I know that some way, somehow, we are going to walk off the field winners."

It had been a long time coming, but the Cowboys were certainly winners now. And the Super Bowl victory gave the Cowboys more than just a championship—it gave them back their good name.

Miami
Dolphins
1972

The Orange Bowl in Miami, Florida, holds 80,010 fans, and on opening day of the Dolphins' 1972 season there wasn't an empty seat in the place. In that land of sun and sand and surf, football was the number one sport.

The proof was all over town. Middle-aged fans wore bright shirts in the Dolphin team colors—aqua, orange, and white. Car bumpers were decorated with stickers proclaiming, "I Am a Dol-Fan." And the Dial-a-Dolphin radio show was getting better ratings than the local disk jockeys. Even the Miami transit system got into the act, repainting the city buses to match Dolphins' uniforms.

There was good reason for all that civic interest. The Miami Dolphins were on the verge of becoming pro football's finest team. Since 1966, when Miami was formed as an expansion club, the Dolphins had moved steadily up in the standings. In 1972 they were hoping to go all the way.

The Dolphins didn't disappoint their boosters in the opener against the Kansas City Chiefs. The temperature was over 100 degrees, but it was the Dolphins—and not the blazing sun—that made things hot for the Chiefs.

In every phase of the game, the Miami team had the manpower. When the Dolphins got the ball, they showed their muscle. In all of pro football, no team had better runners. Miami had three backs who ran defenses crazy. Inside or outside, the Dolphins could lug the ball for yardage.

Larry Csonka (pronounced Zonka) was Miami's big man—in more ways than one. At 6-foot-3 and 235 pounds, he was an old-fashioned straight-ahead runner. When Csonka had the ball, he moved it. Head lowered, he bulled his way through the enemy lines. Csonka racked up impressive yardage in that manner, but he paid his dues for every inch he gained. Indeed, Csonka had his nose broken regularly and suffered frequent concussions and broken bones. But it took more than pain to stop him. In fact, he once refused to leave a game until he began bleeding in a huddle. Even then, it took some persuasion. The man was tough.

So was Jim Kiick (5-foot-11, 214 pounds). Like Csonka, he was built for heavy duty. He could give and take a blow. When Csonka carried the ball, Kiick was right in the thick of things, blocking like a demon. And when Kiick led the interference, would-be tacklers fell by the wayside. Kiick was no slouch with the ball either. He ran with the same bone-crunching thoroughness that characterized Csonka. Kiick would just as soon run through a man as run around him.

By 1972 Csonka and Kiick had become the most head-rattling runners in the game. But they were only part of the Miami ground attack—as Kansas City soon discovered. For the Dolphins also had the speedy Eugene Morris. Nicknamed "Mercury" for the fleet-footed way he eluded opposing defenses, the 5-foot-10, 190-pound Morris was the breakaway element in the Miami game. Mercury Morris was a hard man to get a hold of.

Not surprisingly, Miami used the running game on its opening drive against Kansas City. The run was to the Dolphins what the pass had been to the Super Joe Jets—the most reliable way of making yardage. The Dolphin attack was geared to the ground game, and Miami had the men to make it work.

First Csonka would bang into the Chiefs' line, going full force, loosening men's grips. Then Morris would slither away from tacklers and break into the secondary, where he was always a threat to go for the touchdown.

With a boom and a whir, the Dolphins moved the ball. Of course, Csonka and Morris had plenty of help from their teammates. When All-Pro guard Larry Little pulled out of the line to lead a running play, he was an impressive sight. Little was big, and he was quick—so quick that he once ran the 40-yard dash in 4.9 seconds.

Mercury Morris, the Miami speedster, runs with the ball.

When he came to the NFL as a free agent with San
Diego, Little's speed made the Chargers want to try him
at fullback. With Miami, however, he was simply the
best blocking guard in the game. Led by Little, the
Dolphin line made the Kansas City defense look like
Swiss cheese—full of holes. And through those holes
came the Dolphin runners.

Quarterback Bob Griese called the plays for Miami.
A cool tactician, Griese didn't have Namath's flair for
the bomb, or Staubach's for the scramble. But he knew
how to keep the ball moving. Griese could run, throw,
do it all. And always he worked with a quiet assertive-
ness, a thorough professionalism. When he had the
Chiefs looking for the run, Griese switched to the pass.
And just like that, Miami had a touchdown—a 14-yard
pass to Marlin Briscoe. Briscoe, one of the Dolphins'
many fine pass catchers, wasn't even a starter. He was
playing for the injured Howard Twilley.

From the run to the pass and back again to the
run—Griese kept the Kansas City defense off balance
all day. And in the blistering heat Csonka and company
ran the Chiefs into the ground. Csonka toted the ball 21
times that day for a total gain of 118 yards.

Twice he got the ball close enough for Miami
place-kicker Garo Yepremian to boot field goals of 47
and 15 yards. In Yepremian, the Dolphins had a
sure-footed kicker. Back in Cyprus, where he was born,
Yepremian had been a fine soccer player. Just 5-foot-8
and 175 pounds, he was an unlikely-looking football

player. At Detroit, where he played before coming to Miami, he had never been accepted by the veterans, who didn't consider him a "real" football player. But in Miami, anyone who could kick with his kind of accuracy, was more than welcome.

With a "toe" like Yepremian's on the roster, a team could rely on playing for field position. And that was the approach Miami took. The Dolphins were basically a ball-control team. On offense they relied on running the football. And on defense they just went out and got it.

There was nothing fancy about the Dolphin defense. It didn't have a fancy name like other defensive units, and it wasn't well publicized. The Miami defense may not have made much of an impression on newspaper men, but it certainly impressed the Chiefs. Operating out of what Miami called the "Fifty-three defense," the Dolphins made life difficult for Len Dawson, the shrewd Chief quarterback. Fifty-three was Bob Matheson's number, and Matheson was a rover who sometimes played as a linebacker, or as a defensive end, depending on the situation.

When Matheson dropped to the linebacker spot, Miami was relying on only three men to rush the passer and stop running plays up the middle. Meanwhile, Matheson could offer an extra hand on short pass coverage and wide running plays.

That afternoon against the Dolphins, Dawson couldn't understand why Matheson shifted to linebacker. As the Kansas City quarterback said later,

"With a three-man rush, they had eight people back on pass defense. The most receivers you send out is five, so they're doubled up on most everybody out there."

Dawson finally figured out what the Dolphins were up to—the hard way. When he tried to pass, Miami defensive back Jake Scott intercepted the ball and set up a Csonka two-yard touchdown plunge. The combination of a relentless offense and an imaginative defense earned the Dolphins their first victory, 20–10.

For Miami coach Don Shula it was a satisfying win. The Dolphins' precision play reflected the coach's highly organized system. Shula's practice sessions were noted for their meticulous planning. Said offensive line coach Monte Clark, "Everything is laid out to the minute, like four and a half minutes here, eighteen minutes there."

Even as a player, Shula had been a thinker on the field. When he played cornerback for Weeb Ewbank at Baltimore, Shula called defensive signals, a job usually given to linebackers. As a coach at Miami, Shula's strategic genius earned him the respect of his players, and there was little of the resentment that had marked his last year at Baltimore. Shula was just as tough with his players—but the Dolphins, unlike the Colts, were winning. And a winning team will gladly take the bad with the good.

Said Yepremian, "He's the kind of guy who knows when to pat you on the back and when to put you down. Even if I miss a kick, he says, 'Keep your head up. You'll get the next one.' But one day he caught me doing something I shouldn't have, punting on the practice field, and he got on me quick."

Added Csonka, "He doesn't give you big fines if you're late or something. He humiliates you a little bit and makes you feel as if you've let the whole team down. But he also creates great fellowship on this team by treating everybody alike."

Shula treated the Dolphins like winners, and that's what they looked like when they faced the Houston Oilers the next week. On the slick artificial turf of the Houston Astrodome, Miami ran roughshod over the Texas bunch. The mean Miami machine rolled right over the Oilers. Within 25 minutes the Dolphins had scored 20 points. Morris (94 yards), Csonka (79), and Kiick (55) were virtually unstoppable as Miami racked up a 34–13 victory.

Of course it wasn't a hotly contested game. Houston was not really a pro power. A tougher test came next, against the Minnesota Vikings—a team that appeared to be just as fierce as Miami. Minnesota jumped to an early lead on a 56-yard touchdown pass from Viking quarterback Fran Tarkenton to John Gilliam. When Alan Page blocked a Miami field-goal attempt midway through the first quarter, it was clear Miami was in for a fight. Neither team was able to score in the second quarter, so at half time Minnesota still led 7–0.

Then the Miami defense—which was becoming known as the No-Name gang—went to work. Corner-back Tim Foley intercepted the football on Minnesota's

Surrounded by Vikings, quarterback Bob Griese looks for a receiver.

first drive of the second half. Yepremian put the Dolphins back in the game with a field goal from 38 yards out. Minutes later Garo was back again—this time with a three-pointer from 42 yards that narrowed the Viking lead to 7–6.

But then the Vikings began their drive. For six straight minutes Tarkenton kept the attack going. The scrappy Viking quarterback mixed the pass and run artfully. Bill Brown's touchdown from one yard out increased Minnesota's lead to 14–6. And time was running out for Miami.

With less than five minutes remaining, the Dolphins had the ball just inside the midfield stripe. On a fourth down and long yardage, Shula had three options: punt, pass, or kick for the three. The coach decided to send Yepremian in. The little kicker booted his third field goal of the day—from 51 yards away. Minnesota 14, Miami 9.

Now there was only 4:15 to go, and Miami was in trouble. If Tarkenton could mount another time-consuming attack Minnesota would win the game. But the No-Namers weren't about to let that happen. They stood firm, and the Vikings were forced to punt.

And then Griese went to work. It took him just five plays to move the ball all the way down to the Minnesota 3. It was a remarkable effort, but unless Miami could score, it would count for nothing. Only a touchdown would put the Dolphins ahead. Under pressure and against a defensive unit that was as physical as any in pro ball, a three-yard gain would be as hard to get as three miles.

Csonka, Kiick, and Mercury Morris were ready to try, but Griese made other plans. Instead of trying to run the ball, he threw it to Jim Mandich, a sure-fingered emergency pass catcher, who was often used on key passing plays. Mandich did his job, catching the ball in heavy traffic for a touchdown—and a 16–14 comeback win. It was a remarkable performance against the tough, disciplined Vikings.

It was no time to crow about great games, though. For Joe Willie and the Jets were next. Just two weeks before, Namath had had one of his most incredible games. Against the Colts, he'd thrown the football for 496 yards and four touchdowns.

Against Miami, Namath started off hot. On the Jets' first drive he took them all the way to a touchdown with a run-heavy attack. But then Miami took charge. Here came Csonka and Morris, powering their way past mean green-clad Jet tacklers. Then Griese went to Howard Twilley on the pass. Twilley, the experts said, was too small and too slow to be a pro pass catcher, but Twilley had an uncanny ability to get free from tacklers. Now he showed what he could do, grabbing the football on a 16-yard touchdown throw.

The Jets stayed close, but the third quarter ended with Miami ahead 17–10. Then Kiick—always a threat near the goal line—ran the ball from three yards out to give Miami a little insurance. The Jets kept trying, but

Reserve quarterback Earl Morrall (15) hands off to Larry Csonka.

the game ended with the Dolphins in front 27–17.

After four games the team was still undefeated. But before they could get overconfident, bad luck struck the Dolphins. Against their next opponents, the San Diego Chargers, Griese rolled out to pass to Kiick early in the game. Charger lineman Ron East dove and grabbed Griese's right ankle. The foot was planted in artificial turf and did not "give." The result was a broken ankle. The injured Griese was carried off the field.

Reserve quarterback Earl Morrall came in to finish the game. At Baltimore, under Shula, Morrall had bailed the Colts out when Unitas was injured. Earl was a little older now—at 38 he was ten years older than the average Dolphin—but he still had plenty to offer. Shula had gotten Morrall for a $100 waiver price from Baltimore—an insult to the aging veteran. Coming off the bench to face the Chargers, Morrall showed what a bargain Shula had come up with. Earl did not falter— nor did Miami.

The No-Name defense did its part. Miami safety Dick Anderson picked up a fumble and ran it 35 yards for a touchdown. Then cornerback Lloyd Mumphord intercepted a pass, which Morrall converted into another Dolphin TD with a fine pass to Twilley. Before the game ended, Morrall threw another touchdown pass—this one to Paul Warfield. Earl Morrall, the quarterback no one had wanted, led the Dolphins to a 24–10 win.

It was tougher going against Buffalo—a team Miami

normally scored well against. But this time the Dolphins came undone early in the game. With a 7–3 lead, Morrall got into trouble. First he threw a pass to Morris that bounced off Mercury's helmet and into the hands of the Bills' Ken Lee. Lee ran 16 yards for the touchdown that put Buffalo ahead 10–7.

Then Morrall shuttled the ball to Morris again, and Mercury dropped it. Buffalo's Don Croft fell on it, and the officials ruled that Morris had fumbled a forward lateral. Shula was so enraged by that decision that he came off the sidelines to argue the point. In the "discussion" that followed, Shula nudged the official, and a penalty was called against Miami. Then a Buffalo field goal gave the Bills a 13–7 lead at the half.

In the third quarter the Dolphins got down to business. Miami's tackle Manny Fernandez got through the blocking line so quickly that he beat Buffalo's running back Wayne Patrick to the hand-off. The Dolphins got the ball—and the Zonk got a touchdown on the very next play. Later in the quarter, Yepremian kicked a field goal, and Miami led 17–13.

Miami seemed to have the game well in hand, but Buffalo was not the pushover it had been in the past. The Bills fought on. With 1:07 remaining, they narrowed the count to 24–23. But time was on the Dolphins' side, and Miami squeaked through with its sixth straight victory. It was only by one point, but the Dolphins had won and that was what counted.

Even on an off day, Miami had had enough poise to

hang in there. It was the mark of a winner. Of course, the Dolphins had more than spirit going for them. The team was also deep and gifted. Even without Griese, Miami ran smoothly. Morrall may have had an off day against Buffalo, but he was back to normal against his old mates, the Baltimore Colts. The 39-year-old Unitas had been banished to the Colt bench. But Earl Morrall was out there leading the way for the Dolphins.

Morrall's old hand still had some magic in it. He got the attack going, throwing a short completion to Warfield. And then Zonk and Mercury Morris began running the ball. The fine blocking of Larry Little and Bob Kuechenberg gave them plenty of running room—and Csonka and Morris thundered through. Csonka scored Miami's first touchdown from the 2-yard line.

Then Baltimore gained possession—but not for long. When the Dolphins got the ball back, Morrall helped them take it all the way. First the old crew-cut, in familiar jersey number 15, hit Kiick with a pass for seven yards. Then he called for a bit of razzle dazzle. Morrall dropped back to pass the ball, and threw to Briscoe. As soon as Briscoe caught the ball, he lateraled to Warfield, who was racing by him in a play known as the "flea-flicker." Warfield caught the ball and ran 26 yards. Then Csonka carried it in from the one for the touchdown.

And so it went with Miami and Morrall. The veteran quarterback completed 9 of 15 passes to lead the Dolphins to a 23–0 shutout. The Dolphins' defensive stand-out was middle linebacker Nick Buoniconti. Considered too small for his position at 5-foot-11 and 220 pounds, Buoniconti had had to prove himself throughout his career. What he lacked in size, Buoniconti more than made up for in quickness. He was under particular pressure in the Dolphins' "53" defense, but he was quickly gaining recognition as one of the league's great linebackers.

In a rematch against Buffalo the next week, Miami figured to win big this time. But again the Bills were stubborn foes, refusing to give an inch. The Dolphins were ahead 16–13 when the turning point came. A Miami drive was stalled when Buffalo defensive tackle Jerry Patton complained that the referee had given Miami a few inches more than it deserved. The matter would have been trivial, but Patton argued too loudly and too long. Finally the official called a penalty for unsportsmanlike conduct, giving the Dolphins 15 yards and a crucial first down.

The Dolphins went on to score a touchdown. After that Buffalo seemed to lose heart, and the Dolphins surged ahead. Mercury Morris outgained the great O.J. Simpson with 106 yards, and Miami went on to a 30–16 win.

Against the New England Patriots, their next opponents, Miami was unstoppable. In fact, the first five times the Dolphins got the ball, they were able to put points on the scoreboard. Here was Morris, streaking into the secondary, gliding like a hockey player in his

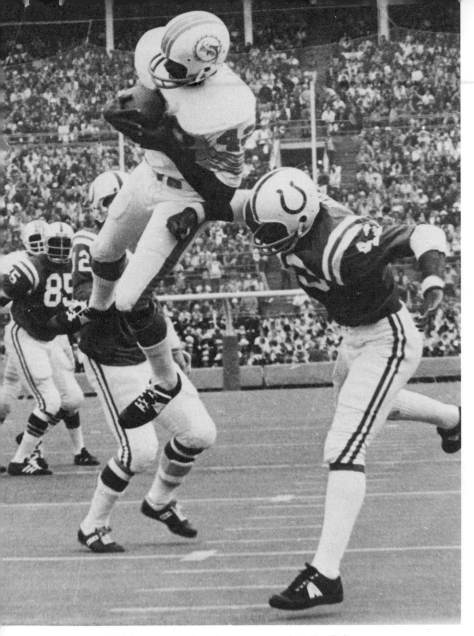

Paul Warfield leaps up and grabs a pass against the Colts.

regulation cleats. He scored the opening touchdown—and the next one. Morrall made it look easy too, throwing to Otto Stowe for 49 yards. Later he hit another touchdown pass, this time to Briscoe.

In every phase of football, Miami was brilliant that afternoon. Even third-string quarterback Jim Del Gaizo made things hot for the Patriots. When Morrall sat down for a breather, Del Gaizo came in and completed four of six passes for 145 yards and two touchdowns.

It was a long day for the Patriots, but when the clock finally ran down, the scoreboard read: Miami 52, New England 0. That marked the Dolphins' ninth straight victory. It was also the 100th victory in Shula's coaching career.

The Dolphins next opponents, the New York Jets, put up a much stronger fight. Morrall got off to a good start, hitting Twilley for a nine-yard touchdown. But the Jets came roaring back. Namath's passing was right on target, and by half time, Joe and the Jets had run up a 17–14 lead.

But it was not the first time the Dolphins had been behind in a game. And under Morrall, they rallied. In fact, the veteran quarterback ran the ball himself for 31 yards and a touchdown.

Still, the New Yorkers came storming back. Joe Willie led them, showing the strong arm that a few years back had made the Jets world champions. This time it got them into the end zone on a four-yard pass to Wayne Stewart—and into the lead, 24–21.

Miami refused to be beaten, though. Calmly, Morrall set the mighty Dolphin forces in action. Csonka and Morris banged through the fierce Jet line. No easy yards there—but they moved the ball anyway. Csonka thundered through like a wounded rhino, his big legs pumping, his strong body wrenching violently away from the Jet tacklers. Sometimes he carried two or three men with him just to gain another yard or so.

When Csonka didn't carry, Mercury Morris did. Moving inside or outside, Morris was a threat. Everyone knew how fast he could move, but the elusive Mercury had more than speed going for him. As strong as he was fast, Morris could bench press more weight than any man on the Dolphin squad. He had more than one way of getting by tacklers. And in the fading minutes of the game he used all his powers. The Dolphins moved downfield, methodically grinding out the yardage.

Down to the Jets' 10-yard line came the Dolphins. And once again, Morrall gave the ball to Morris. Mercury exploded through the line, making tricky cuts that left Jet tacklers clutching at thin air. He left a trail of tacklers behind as he zigzagged his way for the touchdown. The Dolphins had done it again—Miami 28, New York 24.

The victory, the Dolphins' tenth in a row, assured Miami of a spot in the playoffs. It also provoked talk of the Dolphins going unbeaten through the season, a feat accomplished only twice before in the NFL. In 1934 the

Chicago Bears had been 13–0, and in 1942 the Bears did it again, going 11–0.

If the 1972 Dolphins wanted to be the third team to go undefeated, they couldn't let up for a minute. And they didn't. In the final games of the season, the Dolphins went all-out . . .

Miami 31	St. Louis 10
Miami 37	New England 21
Miami 23	New York Giants 13
Miami 16	Baltimore 0

Playing the way they had all year, the Dolphins finished the season with a 14–0 record. Along the way they racked up some other pretty impressive statistics. On offense, Miami's total of 2,960 yards rushing broke the previous record held by the 1934 Chicago Bears. In regular-season play Csonka gained 1,117 yards, Morris had 1,000, and Kiick 521.

The defense, of course, couldn't be overlooked either. Although they were a man shy up front, the three-man line of Fernandez, Den Herder, and Stanfill sacked opposing quarterbacks 33 times during the season. And while they were still known as the No-Name defense, men like Nick Buoniconti, Kolen, Doug Swift, Matheson, Scott, Anderson, Foley and Curtis Johnson were no longer unknown to pro football fans. Opposing teams averaged little more than one touchdown a game against the rugged Miami defense.

Miami had all that—and Yepremian too. The little

balding kicker had proved a real asset to Miami. From 1970, when he joined the team as a free agent, he had made roughly three of every four field-goal attempts. From 39 yards and under, he was practically flawless. In his first three seasons at Miami, Yepremian made 49 of 56 field goals from that distance.

Overall, Miami was as close to the perfect football team as a man could find. Fast and smart, it had shown poise and precision through a regular-season schedule of 14 games. Fortunately, the Dolphins were also deep in manpower. They had to be in the AFC playoff game against the Cleveland Browns.

When Mercury Morris injured his foot during that game, the Dolphins still had Jim Kiick to turn to. But before the Dolphins could get the ball to Kiick, they had to fight to stay in the game. Cleveland was not exactly bowled over by the perfect history Miami had managed in regular-season play.

Even the Dolphins knew that their 14–0 record meant nothing if they flopped in the money games. And for a while, it looked as if they might. Miami led early in the game, but in the fourth quarter the fighting Browns came back. A 27-yard pass from Cleveland quarterback Mike Phipps to Fair Hooker gave the Browns a 14–13 lead.

With some eight minutes left to play, Miami got the ball at its own 45. On first down Cleveland blitzed Morrall, but Morrall was cool under fire. He lofted a pass to Paul Warfield, who was racing downfield with

Jim Kiick (21) scores against Cleveland in the AFC playoffs.

his silky strides, just behind Cleveland's Ben Davis.

Into the air sprang Warfield, jumping high. He bobbled the ball in midair, but regained it as he fell to the ground at the 20. It was a spectacular catch, but it knocked the wind out of Warfield for a moment. He rested for one play, but there was too much at stake to watch the game from the sidelines. When Warfield came back to the game he didn't have to repeat his heroics. The mere threat of the man was enough to intimidate the Browns. For when Warfield went out on the next play, Cleveland linebacker Bill Andrews, seeing him streak to the end zone, interfered with his progress —a rules infraction that moved the ball to the 8-yard line.

Then it was Kiick's turn. After several seasons as a starter, Kiick had been forced to share his running back position with Morris. Kiick hadn't liked the idea and had said so. But now, when it counted, he was ready to play. From the 8, he went barreling through the Brown line. Slamming violently into tacklers, he somehow managed to stay on his feet, going all the way for the touchdown. That gave Miami a 20–14 victory and their 15th straight win.

But the Dolphins weren't home free yet. They still had to play the Pittsburgh Steelers for the AFC championship. The game would be played in Pittsburgh, where the fans were so noisy that football players could hardly hear their quarterback's signals. The Steelers—and their fans—would be hard to beat.

As running back John (Frenchy) Fuqua put it: "When you come to Pittsburgh, you are playing forty players and fifty thousand fans."

The Dolphins did, in fact, have trouble getting started against the charged-up Steelers. Morrall did his best, but it had been a long season for the aging quarterback. By the end of the first half, Miami was trailing 10–7.

Morrall had brought the Dolphins this far, but Griese was mended and in uniform. Shula did not let sentiment dictate strategy when Earl had trouble getting the attack going. He decided to start Griese in the second half.

It was a good decision. Led by Griese, the Dolphins really began to move. Larry Little, Bob Kuechenberg and Norm Evans toppled Steeler after Steeler to give Csonka and Kiick some running room. And the two big Dolphins thundered through for 80 yards, with Kiick making the final two for the touchdown. Now Miami led 14–10.

The Steelers attempted a field goal in the fourth quarter, but Miami blocked the kick and took possession at the Steeler 49. And again, the Dolphins drove. Bang, bang—through the holes went Csonka and Kiick again, twisting, stretching for the extra yard or two. During the eleven-play drive, Griese passed only once. Csonka and Kiick were not to be stopped. And down near the goal line, it was Kiick who did it again, scoring from the 3. Miami went on to win the championship and their 16th straight game, 21–17.

No team had ever run up a string of victories like that. Yet some football experts were less than overwhelmed by the Dolphins. In fact, most of them (including the country's most famous fan, President Richard M. Nixon) picked the Washington Redskins to beat Miami in the Super Bowl.

As columnist Paul Zimmerman wrote in the *New York Post*:

> Miami's opponents, collectively, had the worst percentage in football (.375). Which doesn't mean that 16–0 isn't an impressive achievement given the emotional ups and downs of professional football. . . .
>
> It just means that, well, that Miami wrapped it up early and went to sleep for a month and woke up only twice—when they got in trouble against Pittsburgh and Cleveland on the way to the AFC title.

Against Miami came the red-hot Redskins whose teams played with the spirit of high schoolers. Even after they had a game won, the Redskins were still trying to hurt people. After victories, the Redskin players would actually break into cheers—rare behavior in the pro game.

Miami didn't need to get psyched up that way. On Super Sunday it was apparent that the Dolphins had come to play. And play they did. The No-Names—led by the front three of Fernandez, Stanfill, and Den Herder—never allowed the Skins' league-leading run-

Miami's mighty defense converges on Charley Harraway in the Super Bowl.

ning back, Larry Brown, to get going. He managed only 72 yards in 22 carries. Before 86,000 sweltering fans in the smog-enveloped Los Angeles Coliseum, the No-Names made the vaunted Washington running game look just ordinary.

The Skins, however, were unable to contain the Miami offense. Csonka did what Brown couldn't do. He gained 112 yards, just nine short of the Super Bowl record set by New York's Matt Snell in 1969. Brown's longest run was for eleven yards; Csonka's was for 49 yards. That run was the longest one managed against the tough Washington defense all season. In the air Griese completed eight of eleven passes for 88 yards and a touchdown to Twilley. It was a brilliant performance, especially for someone who had been injured for much of the season. But Griese played as though he had never been away.

And if President Nixon was disappointed as he watched the 14–7 Dolphin victory on television in Key Biscayne, Florida, up in Miami, Dolphin fans rejoiced. In that football-crazy city, the air was filled with sounds of firecrackers, horns and thousands of voices chanting, "We're Number 1!"

For Don Shula and the Dolphins it was a great way to end a 17–0 season. Just perfect, in fact.

Index